SCRIPTURE, SACRAMENTS, SPIRITUALITY

For Jim O'Keefe
The staff and students of Ushaw College
And my friends in the North East

SCRIPTURE
SACRAMENTS
SPIRITUALITY

Michael T. Winstanley SDB

McCrimmons
Great Wakering, Essex

First published in United Kingdom in 2002
by MCCRIMMON PUBLISHING CO. LTD.
10-12 High Street, Great Wakering, Essex, SS3 0EQ
Email: mccrimmons@dial.pipex.com Website: www.mccrimmons.com

ISBN 0 85597 639 X

British Library Cataloguing in Publication Data.
A catalogue record for this book is available from the British Library.

Acknowledgements

Scripture quotations are from the NRSV unless otherwise indicated.

New Revised Standard Version Bible: Anglicized Edition, copyright 1989, 1995, Division of Christian Education of the National Council of the Churches of Christ in the United States of America. Used by permission. All rights reserved.

Other scripture quotations are from:

New English Bible © Oxford University Press and Cambridge University Press 1961, 1970. Used with permission.

New Jerusalem Bible published and copyright 1966, 1967, 1968 and 1974 by Darton Longman and Todd Ltd, and used by permission of the publishers.

Extracts from *Resurrection People*, D. Catchpole published and copyright 2000 by Darton Longman and Todd Ltd, and used by permission of the publishers; extracts from *Come and See*, M.T. Winstanley, published and copyright 1985 by Darton Longman and Todd Ltd, and used by permission of the publishers; extracts from *Rule for a New Brother* published and copyright 1973 by Darton Longman and Todd Ltd, and used by permission of the publishers.

Extracts from *Guilt and Grace*, P. Tournier, published by Hodder and Stoughton, London, 1962. Reproduced by permission of Hodder and Stoughton Limited.

Extracts from *Into Your Hands* by Michael T. Winstanley, published and copyright St. Paul Publications, Australia, 1993. Reproduced by permission.

Extracts from *The Epistle to the Galatians* by F.F. Bruce, © Paternoster Publishing, 1982. Used with permission.

Extracts from *The Son of Man in Mark*, M.Hooker, and *Jesus and the Victory of God*, N. T. Wright, published by SPCK Publishing, London. Used by permission.

Cover and text design by Nick Snode
Main body text set in Concorde Roman 10/13pt
Heading set in New Baskerville Roman 32pt
Printed and bound by Black Bear Press Ltd., Cambridge, UK

Contents

Introduction

Amongst the developments in the life of the Church in recent years there are two which I find particularly exciting. There has been a new awakening to the importance of the scriptures for our Christian living, and an intensifying thirst to understand God's word. And there has been enormous growth in the participation of the laity in programmes of sacramental preparation. This book is an attempt to support and encourage these twin developments. Its origin lies in an invitation extended to me last year by the Religious Education Team of the Hexham and Newcastle Diocese to give three evenings on the theme 'Scripture shedding light on the Sacraments', the sacraments question being baptism, confirmation, and reconciliation/eucharist. The enthusiastic response of the participants stimulated me to extend and rework the material and offer it in book form to a wider audience.

The approach which I decided to adopt in the original talks was to ask myself what these sacraments continue to mean for me, and which extracts from scripture, especially the New Testament, underpin, clarify and enliven this meaning. Such an approach, which I have continued to follow for the book, is clearly subjective. Other writers would choose other biblical passages in addition or as alternatives.

As the title suggests, I have three aims in the pages which follow. Firstly, I am interested in exploring the scriptures, especially the New Testament. I would like to share with the reader insights which are now available as a result of modern biblical scholarship. Scriptural texts can be viewed from three complementary perspectives, the literary, the historical and the theological. We shall be examining a wide range of types of literature: creation stories, psalms and prophetic texts from the Old Testament; Gospels, letters and the Acts of the Apostles from the New; and within the Gospels there is a variety of literary forms. We shall also meet a number of different authors with their own literary style and techniques. At times we shall refer to the historical background, and some historical issues will need to be addressed. Our main concern will be to unpack the theological message, to see what the texts tell us about God, about the person and mission of Jesus, about the salvation offered and its link with the sacraments, and about some of the implications of being sacramental people.

Secondly, I wish to use the texts which I have chosen in order to enable us to deepen our appreciation and understanding of the sacraments which we celebrate and live today. There is ample evidence of the celebration of baptism and eucharist in New Testament times, and scripture offers elements of a rich theology. Evidence for confirmation and reconciliation is harder to come by, but there is a wealth of material on the Spirit and on reconciliation taken more broadly, and this has served as a basis for the development of these sacraments over the centuries.

Thirdly, I believe that the scriptural texts which we shall reflect upon offer us a sacramental spirituality. Spirituality I would define as a way of living the Gospel. The presence of the Spirit within our hearts and communities creates an identity, a way of being, a system of attitudes and values and meaning, which give shape to our worldview and lifestyle. In fact, no dimension of existence is excluded. I would like to explore briefly the place of our sacramental experience in the sustaining and development of our spirituality.

Many problems face us as we seek to celebrate these four sacraments in our contemporary world, issues of a practical, pastoral, liturgical or theological nature. For instance, there is debate about the wisdom of admitting to baptism children whose parents are not committed. There are arguments about whether the correct setting for baptism is the Sunday Parish Mass or a private family gathering. Given the historical separation of confirmation from baptism, there is the issue of the most appropriate age for its celebration; whether it should precede first communion or be linked to adolescent maturing. With regard to the celebration of the sacrament of reconciliation, many people question whether individual confession is outdated, and advocate the wider availability of general absolution. Eucharistic celebrations can be beset with such problems as styles of music, translations, ministers, and there is the much more fundamental issue about who is permitted to participate fully.

These are relevant questions, important, and at times painful, issues. Nevertheless, this book is not intended to furnish practical answers, liturgical guidelines, pastoral solutions, a full sacramental theology. Its purpose is to allow the word of God to inform our minds, deepen our understanding, fashion our attitudes and our hearts, so that as individuals and communities we may live our Christian discipleship more fully. It is my firm belief that the scriptures will enlighten us about key values and ideas which are to be borne in mind and upheld as we seek to address burning modern issues. I suspect that we may find new vision and fresh dimensions of challenge.

The three evenings of study and reflection out of which this small volume has grown were attended by people who were, in the main, engaged in helping others to prepare for the celebration of the sacraments. As well as such catechists, it is my hope that many others – teachers, students, future ministers, Christians of all denominations – may find the following pages interesting, instructive and enriching. They are not intended primarily as source material for meetings and discussion, though they may serve that purpose. Rather, I offer them as suggestions for personal study, reflection, and prayer. I am convinced that the more we have pondered God's word and in the light of that word have reflected on the significance of the sacraments in our own life experience, the better we are equipped to be of service to others on their journey.

My love of the scriptures has been nourished over the years by the work of many scholars of different Christian backgrounds. I wish here to express my gratitude to them. In the notes, which I have tried to keep to a minimum, I have attempted to acknowledge the authors on whom I have depended most, and apologise in advance for any omissions which may have occurred. I would like to thank in a special way Prof. Frank Moloney, SDB, Rev. Dr. Sean Hall, Miss Paddy Rylands, Ruth and Eleanor who have patiently read the manuscript and made helpful comments and suggestions, and Sharon O'Donnell at the RE Centre for the initial inspiration. Finally, I thank my community at Savio House and my colleagues at Ushaw College for their support and encouragement.

I dedicate these pages to Fr. Jim O'Keefe, the president of Ushaw College, a good friend and challenging fellow traveller on the road of Christian discipleship, and also to the staff and students of the College, and to all my friends in the North East.

Michael T. Winstanley SDB
Savio House
Bollington

Baptism

THE THEOLOGY OF BAPTISM as it is presented
in the New Testament is extremely rich. In this
chapter I would like to explore a number of
themes through which the scriptures shed light
on this multifaceted source of life and meaning.
By way of introduction we shall examine the
beginning of the apostolic mission in Acts.
We shall then move on to consider the ministry
of John the Baptist and the baptism of Jesus.
Subsequently we shall reflect on the effects of
baptism: our relationship with God, our
oneness in the Risen Jesus, our membership of a
community. Finally we shall focus a little on the
implications of this for our style of living, and
draw our considerations to a conclusion with
the symbol of the 'seal'. Whilst each theme has
its own consistency, there is inevitably some
overlap, some interweaving of strands, some
fluidity. Some aspects will require further
treatment in the following chapter on
confirmation.

The Beginning

AN EXCERPT FROM THE ACTS OF THE APOSTLES provides a useful introduction to the topic. [1] In the Book of Acts Luke includes eight sermons preached by Peter, the leading spokesman and witness, and nine by Paul, the missionary to the Gentiles. They follow the same basic format, and whilst having roots in the early tradition, bear the hallmarks of Lucan composition. In the first sermon, which inaugurates the ministry of the Church and is given immediately after the Pentecost event, Peter speaks about Jesus, who in his ministry was commended by God through the miracles and signs he worked amongst the people, and who was put to death by crucifixion. But God raised him from death to sit at his right hand in power. As a result of this, the Spirit has been outpoured. Peter professes Jesus as Lord and Christ. This is, in fact, an excellent summary of the early Christian kerygma or proclamation, the foundation of our faith. However, it is the description of the reaction to this apostolic discourse and Peter's subsequent response which are particularly informative for our theme. The story line reads as follows:

> [37] Now when they heard this, they were cut to the heart and said to Peter and to the other apostles, "Brothers, what should we do?" [38] Peter said to them, "Repent, and be baptised every one of you in the name of Jesus Christ so that your sins may be forgiven; and you will receive the gift of the Holy Spirit. [39] For the promise is for you, for your children, and for all who are far away, everyone whom the Lord our God calls to him." [40] And he testified with many other arguments and exhorted them, saying, "Save yourselves from this corrupt generation." [41] So those who welcomed his message were baptised, and that day about three thousand persons were added (Acts 2:37-41).

Several interesting points emerge from Peter's response to the people's anguished question about what they should do. Firstly, there is the need to 'repent', a demand made by Jesus too in his proclamation of the advent of the Kingdom of God (Mark 1:15). The word does not mean simply saying "I'm sorry". It signifies something far-reaching and radical. The term in question, *metanoia*, really means to change one's mind, outlook, way of thinking, agenda, and this implies a change of lifestyle and direction. People must turn away from sinfulness, and return wholeheartedly to the God who in Jesus approaches them with the offer of salvation.

Secondly, there is the demand that they be baptised in the name of Jesus Christ for the forgiveness of sins. The gift of forgiveness was one of the principal aspects of God's awaited intervention to establish the Kingdom, the sign that Israel's exile was really over (Jeremiah 31:31-34; 33:4-11; Isaiah 52-55; Ezekiel 36:24-26,33). [2] The forgiving of sins through his authoritative word and through the welcome of his table fellowship was therefore central to the ministry of Jesus. It was a key sign of the dawning new age. However, in his ministry Jesus does not seem to have linked the gift of forgiveness explicitly with baptism. This link, now made by Peter, has echoes of the approach used by John the Baptist. The forgiveness which Peter claims to be available through the death and resurrection of Jesus demands that his hearers acknowledge their need for forgiveness, and that they trust that the Risen Jesus has power to communicate that forgiveness.

Thirdly, baptism takes place *'in the name of Jesus'*. This probably means that the procedure entailed speaking Jesus' name and confessing him to be 'the Christ' (Messiah), or 'the Lord', or 'the Son of God', titles which enshrined the faith insight of his post-resurrection followers. In his ministry Jesus claimed a unique role in the establishing of the Kingdom of God. In the proclamation of the early Church Jesus is central, and the identity of his followers is established by what they believe and profess about him.

Fourthly, Peter is inviting people to make a visible and open profession of their acceptance of Jesus. At the same time, they are being invited to 'join up', to become members of the group of his followers. Jesus' choice of the twelve during his ministry was symbolic; it indicated his intention to reconstitute Israel around himself as the true, restored people of God, the people embraced by the Kingdom. What Peter is doing reflects the typically Jewish way of viewing things, whereby God chooses and saves a people. God through Jesus is now creating a new people, a new covenant community. Membership of this newly constituted group is crucial for salvation.

And fifthly, in conjunction with submission to the ritual of water baptism, Peter promises the gift of the Spirit, that Spirit which has already been bestowed on the twelve. Peter's exhortation is directed not only to the Jews, but also to *'all who are far away'*, which probably includes the Gentiles too. Their coming to share this experience is described later in Acts (8:38; 10:44-48; 18:8; 19:5-6).

Baptism and Jesus

JOHN THE BAPTIST

THE PRACTICE OF BAPTISM in the early days of Christianity, and its link with the gift of the Spirit were not Peter's brain child. As I have already implied, there was continuity between what Peter was proclaiming and what happened during the ministry of Jesus. Before Jesus embarked upon his mission, the scene was set by the man known popularly as 'the baptiser'. We encounter him at the beginning of Mark's Gospel. (3)

> *1* The beginning of the good news of Jesus Christ, the Son of God. *2* As it is written in the prophet Isaiah, "See, I am sending my messenger ahead of you, who will prepare your way; *3* the voice of one crying out in the wilderness: 'Prepare the way of the Lord, make his paths straight,' " *4* John the baptiser appeared in the wilderness, proclaiming a baptism of repentance for the forgiveness of sins. *5* And people from the whole Judean countryside and all the people of Jerusalem were going out to him, and were baptised by him in the river Jordan, confessing their sins. *6* Now John was clothed with camel's hair, with a leather belt around his

waist, and he ate locusts and wild honey. 7 He proclaimed, "The one who is more powerful than I is coming after me; I am not worthy to stoop down and untie the thong of his sandals. 8 I have baptised you with water; but he will baptise you with the Holy Spirit." (Mark 1:1-8)

The opening verse, echoing the Genesis beginning in order to herald a new beginning, a new creation, expresses Mark's objective and his fundamental faith stance. In writing this document, he sets out to proclaim news to make his readers and hearers glad, the good news which Jesus originally brought, the good news which Jesus has now become. He states clearly right at the outset his firm belief that this Jesus, whose story he is about to narrate, is the Christ (Messiah, anointed one), and the Son of God. These are the two main aspects of Jesus' identity and mission explored throughout the Gospel narrative.

Mark then introduces John, sent by God to prepare the long awaited Day of the Lord, God's decisive intervention in history. The scriptural quotation confirms the divine origin of his mission, and makes it clear that his role is that of a forerunner, setting the scene, paving the way for another who will follow. John's ministry in the wilderness along the Jordan river, a deeply symbolic setting, is characterised by his dramatic preaching and his baptising. Water rituals are widespread in world religions, linked with purification and new life. In the Old Testament there are many prescriptions for ritual washing, and the prophets and psalmists use such washing as a symbol of interior cleansing (Isaiah 1:16; Psalm 51:7). The prophets came to hope for cleansing and renewal at some future date, when God would pour out his spirit on his people like water (Joel 3:1-2; Ezekiel 36: 25-27). In Jesus' time voluntary ritual washing was on the increase amongst the Pharisees and the Qumran community.

There was something special, however, something original about John's baptism. (4) It was different from the self-administered immersion which some scholars believe converts to Judaism were expected to undergo. It differed also from the repeated ritual washing practised in the elite Qumran community, also self-administered. John's baptism was offered to all Jews. It was a one-off event and not repeated. It was not self administered, but administered by him. It stemmed from the recognition that Israel had gone astray, the realisation of the need for conversion, personal and national. There was an urgency about it, because John proclaimed the imminence of the day of reckoning and salvation. Through submitting to John's baptism, people signified their repentance and pledged to live a reformed life. They expressed their hope of escaping the threat of fiery judgement, and of sharing in the great outpouring of God's cleansing, forgiving and life-giving Spirit on the last day.

John recognises the limitations of his baptism, for it is water baptism only, and is preparatory. Another is to come, a mightier one, who will baptise with the Holy Spirit. This will be a sign that the new age of God's salvation has come.

THE BAPTISM OF JESUS

JESUS OF NAZARETH was amongst those who came to be baptised. He associated and identified himself with his sinful people.

> *9* In those days Jesus came from Nazareth of Galilee and was baptised by John in the Jordan. *10* And just as he was coming up out of the water, he saw the heavens torn apart and the Spirit descending like a dove on him. *11* And a voice came from heaven, "You are my Son, the Beloved; with you I am well pleased." *12* And the Spirit immediately drove him out into the wilderness. *13* He was in the wilderness forty days, tempted by Satan; and he was with the wild beasts; and the angels waited on him (Mark 1:9-13).

In Mark's account, it is not the baptism itself which is important but the accompanying phenomena. Firstly, the heavens are *'torn open'*, graphic traditional imagery, which indicates that God is about to communicate (Ezekiel 1:1; Isaiah 24:18; 63:11). The verb is used in Isaiah 64:1 to refer to the moment of eschatological salvation when

God will finally intervene for the deliverance of God's people. The Spirit descends like a dove and rests on Jesus. This may be an echo of the creative Spirit hovering over the waters at the dawn of time (Genesis 1:2), or a reference to Noah's dove at the time of the flood, a harbinger of peace and hope (Genesis 8:11). For the Evangelist, Jesus is anointed with the Spirit, and is empowered for mission. He is the anointed one, the Messiah, the Christ.

The second phenomenon is the voice from heaven which acknowledges Jesus as the Son, uniquely Beloved. The words are thought to be a fusion of two Old Testament texts. There are the words from Psalm 2:7 which were addressed to a new king at his coronation anointing: (*'You are my son; today I have become your Father'*). The other source passage is one of the Servant songs of Isaiah (42:1 – *'Here is my servant whom I behold, my chosen one in whom my Soul delights. I have endowed him with my Spirit that he may bring true justice to the nations'.*) So we are presented with God's normative view of Jesus' identity and role, a view with which that of Mark (1:1) coincides!

In all the Gospels the two outstanding traits of Jesus are his relationship with the Father and his sense of mission. The two are interdependent. Jesus' awareness of the Father's unique love enables him to address God as 'Abba', the term which children used when chattering to dad, but highly unusual as an expression of prayer to God.
It seems to have captured something of his intimacy, trust and unconditional love. His sense of 'being sent' and his commitment to his mission are bound up with this relationship.

It is interesting to observe that the New Testament writers do not explicitly use Jesus' baptism as a model for ours, probably because the fact proved something of an embarrassment for them. (5) But the twin elements of relationship and mission are at the core of the early Church's understanding of baptism. It is perhaps artificial to separate them, but I propose to lay greater emphasis on the mission element later in connection with the sacrament of confirmation.

Relationship with God

In the first place, Christian baptism establishes a new relationship with God.

PAUL

PAUL DESCRIBES THIS RELATIONSHIP in powerful and moving terms in his letters. I offer two particularly striking examples, the first from the letter to the Galatians (4:4-7), the other from that to the Romans (8:14-17). [6]

> *4* But when the fullness of time had come, God sent his Son, born of a woman, born under the law, *5* in order to redeem those who were under the law, so that we might receive adoption as children. *6* And because you are children, God has sent the Spirit of his Son into our hearts, crying, "Abba! Father!" *7* So you are no longer a slave but a child, and if a child then also an heir, through God (Galatians 4:4-7).

> *14* For all who are led by the Spirit of God are children of God. *15* For you did not receive a spirit of slavery to fall back into fear, but you have received a spirit of adoption. When we cry, "Abba! Father!" *16* it is that very Spirit bearing witness with our spirit that we are children of God, *17* and if children, then heirs, heirs of God and joint heirs with Christ – if, in fact, we suffer with him so that we may also be glorified with him (Romans 8:14-17).

Paul describes the basic human situation as a condition of slavery, a state of being (for Jews) under the Law, a context of fear. In Galatians he writes that God has taken the initiative and sent his son into this human and Jewish world in order to set free those enslaved. In parallel, God has sent the Spirit of Jesus into our hearts in that outpouring which accompanies baptism. In both letters Paul proclaims that this redeeming gift transforms us, Jews and Gentiles alike,

from slaves into adoptive children. We are drawn into Jesus' relationship with God. As God's sons and daughters, we can address
God as 'Abba', Father, using that intimate name used by Jesus, which
communicates a sense of "loving nearness and implicit trust". [7]
There was something distinctive about Jesus' use of this family term,
which then became part of the prayer life of Aramaic speaking
Christians, and was preserved in the vocabulary of Greek speaking
Christians too. The ability to cry to God in this way from the depths
of our being is the sign that the Spirit of Jesus dwells within us, and
confirms the reality of our adoption. As fully grown and mature
adopted children, we also come to share the heritage which Christ
has won through his death and resurrection. We are heirs to eternal
life, guaranteed a share in his heavenly glory. All this is the gift of
God, freely bestowed.

JOHN

THE FOURTH EVANGELIST expresses his understanding of this in a
different way. [8] In chapter 3 Nicodemus, a pre-eminent teacher in
Israel and member of the highest governing body, approaches Jesus
by night. He acknowledges that Jesus must come 'from God', given
the signs which he is performing. His introduction seems to be leading up to an important question, but Jesus responds before he can
articulate it.

> *3* Jesus answered him, "Very truly, I tell you, no one can see
> the kingdom of God without being born from above."
> *4* Nicodemus said to him, "How can anyone be born after
> having grown old? Can one enter a second time into the
> mother's womb and be born?" *5* Jesus answered, "Very truly,
> I tell you, no one can enter the kingdom of God without
> being born of water and Spirit." (John 3:3-5)

From a literary point of view, verses 3 and 5 are in carefully balanced
parallel. Both statements of Jesus are solemnly introduced by the typically Johannine double 'Amen' (sometimes translated as 'very truly',

or 'in all truth'). [9] The first statement speaks of seeing the kingdom, the second of entering it. The first speaks of birth from above, the second of birth through water and Spirit. References to the kingdom of God abound in the other Gospels, but are rare in John. The phrase occurs only here, but the kingship theme is central to the passion narrative. The Johannine equivalent, as we shall soon see, is 'eternal life'.

Another literary characteristic of John's Gospel in evidence here is his use of word play, double meanings, and the misunderstanding to which this gives rise. The Greek word (*anothen*) is open to two interpretations. It can mean both 'from above' and also 'again', 'for a second time'. When this kind of thing happens, the interlocutor usually takes the literal or superficial meaning, showing that he or she does not really understand what is at issue. This then enables Jesus to elucidate the true in-depth significance of what he is saying. In this case Nicodemus takes it that Jesus is talking about a second physical birth, and he expresses his surprise. Jesus, however, intends the other meaning of the word – 'from above', and is referring to a birth of a very different order.

This passage also highlights John's two-dimensional vision of things: above/below; heavenly/earthly; Spirit/flesh. There are two contrasting and totally different realms or levels of reality, two spheres of existence. Human beings belong to the lower level, the below, the earthly, the flesh. The gap between the two cannot be bridged by human effort or endeavour. However, in the incarnation the Word of God comes from the 'above', and becomes 'flesh', pitching his tent in our midst (1:14). The life of this Word enfleshed, whose human name is Jesus (1:17), is a journey of return to the Father who sent him, a journey which, when completed, makes it possible for us to participate in the life of the 'above'.

So, to be born 'from above' is to be born of 'water and Spirit'. It is through baptism that we are caught up in the life of the 'above'. Early in the Gospel narrative the Baptist testifies to the fulfilment of what God has indicated to him, namely that *'The one on whom you see the Spirit come down and rest is the one who is to baptise with the*

Holy Spirit' (1:33). Water baptism alone is inadequate. The gift of the Spirit transforms the significance of the water ritual. Through this twofold experience, the gulf between the two spheres is bridged, and the believer enters the kingdom of God. A new quality of life becomes possible for human beings, the very life of God. This kind of life the Evangelist always calls 'eternal life'.

As dialogue becomes discourse Jesus takes this a little further (3:14-17).

> *14* "And just as Moses lifted up the serpent in the wilderness, so must the Son of Man be lifted up, *15* that whoever believes in him may have eternal life. *16* For God so loved the world that he gave his only Son, so that everyone who believes in him may not perish but may have eternal life.
> *17* Indeed, God did not send the Son into the world to condemn the world, but in order that the world might be saved through him." (John 3:14-17)

This extract contains in v.16 the most celebrated expression of the Fourth Gospel, which sums up the whole Christian message of salvation. It is the Gospel in a nutshell. Behind everything stands the love of God, his free initiative and gift. Again we see John's use of synonymous parallelism in verses 16 and 17, as he articulates the consequence of God's love. For God gives/sends His Son, His only Son. That giving/sending is for the benefit of the whole wide world. The purpose of that giving/sending is expressed twice in antithetical terms, negatively and positively. It is that believers should not perish, or be destroyed or be judged (condemned); rather that they should have 'eternal life', be saved.

As I said earlier, rather than use the terms kingdom or salvation, John prefers 'eternal life' (17 times). This is not to be understood mainly as everlasting life, a kind of life which starts only when normal earthly life ends in death. It is a qualitatively different kind of life, the life which pertains to the 'above', the heavenly realm; it is the life of God. It does therefore have an everlasting dimension. But the Fourth Evangelist stresses that 'eternal life' is not a future dream only; it is a present reality. Already, now, believers come to share the life of the beyond. And death cannot snuff out this quality of life. It continues through death and reaches fulfilment beyond the grave. The Prologue states that *'to those who did accept him he gave power to become children of God'* (1:12-13). We become God's children, we are caught up in God's life, through baptism, through birth by water and Spirit.

Another significant facet of the above quotation is found in v.14, namely the image of the Son of Man being 'lifted up'. This verb, which is used of the Servant in Isaiah 52:13, has two levels of meaning. It can indicate to lift up physically, like Moses lifting aloft the bronze serpent in the desert incident as a source of healing and salvation for those bitten by the fiery serpents (Numbers 21:8-9). It can therefore apply to Jesus' crucifixion, his being lifted up on the cross. The verb also means to exalt, to glorify; and so can be used of the resurrection/ascension, the return of Jesus to the Father's side. Whereas in the other New Testament traditions the cross is the low point, the nadir moment dramatically reversed by the resurrection, for John the cross is the high point, the supreme moment of revelation and life-giving. The same word covers both aspects of this mystery. So, 'eternal life', salvation, entry into the Kingdom, become possible because of the death and exaltation of Jesus. Then it is that Jesus, returned to the Father, can send the Spirit. Through water and Spirit we can be born anew and become God's children.

Relationship with the Death and Resurrection of Jesus

PAUL

ANOTHER ASPECT OF BAPTISM switches the emphasis from our relationship with the Father and focuses on our relationship with Christ Jesus, linking baptism with his death and resurrection. I have chosen two passages as illustrations of this (Romans 6:3-6; Ephesians 2:4-6).

3 Do you not know that all of us who have been baptised into Christ Jesus were baptised into his death? *4* Therefore we have been buried with him by baptism into death, so that, just as Christ was raised from the dead by the glory of the Father, so we too might walk in newness of life. *5* For if we have been united with him in a death like his, we will certainly be united with him in a resurrection like his. *6* We know that our old self was crucified with him so that the body of sin might be destroyed, and we might no longer be enslaved to sin. *7* For whoever has died is freed from sin. *8* But if we have died with Christ, we believe that we will also live with him. *9* We know that Christ, being raised from the dead, will never die again; death no longer has dominion over him. *10* The death he died, he died to sin, once for all; but the life he lives, he lives to God. *11* So you also must consider yourselves dead to sin and alive to God in Christ Jesus (Romans 6:3-11).

In this extract from the letter to the Romans, Paul tells us that through baptism – the symbolism refers to immersion – the old self, the child of the first Adam, oriented to sin, is crucified with Jesus, suffers death and is buried. Our sinfulness and the slavery it entails are destroyed. Through the resurrection of Jesus we are raised to freedom and begin to walk in newness of life. We come alive in a new way, alive to God 'in Christ Jesus'. This phrase is Paul's preferred way of expressing our intimate sharing in the resurrected life of Christ. Elsewhere, he writes that he has been crucified with Christ, so that now Christ is alive in him (Galatians 2:19-20).

4 But God, who is rich in mercy, out of the great love with which he loved us *5* even when we were dead through our trespasses, made us alive together with Christ – by grace you have been saved – *6* and raised us up with him and seated us with him in the heavenly places in Christ Jesus (Ephesians 2:4-6).

The letter to the Ephesians puts this slightly differently. (10) Entirely through the free gift of God's merciful love, without any merit or effort on our part (1:6; 2:8-9), we are raised from the death of sinfulness, hopelessness and alienation (see Romans 5:8). In raising and exalting Jesus the Christ, God brings us to life with him, and in this achieves our salvation (see Colossians 2:11-13). We come to be included in the event of Christ's resurrection. Through baptism we begin this new form of existence, we live 'in Christ'; Christ is now the ground of our being. We are God's adopted children (1:5).

JOHN

THIS ONENESS WITH THE RISEN JESUS is illustrated by John through the image of the vine and branches.

> 5 I am the vine, you are the branches. Those who abide in me and I in them bear much fruit, because apart from me you can do nothing.
>
> 9 As the Father has loved me, so I have loved you; abide in my love. 10 If you keep my commandments, you will abide in my love, just as I have kept my Father's commandments and abide in his love (John 15:5, 9-10).

Branches depend on and draw life from the vine. Separated from the vine, they wither and die. Similarly, believers are grafted onto the vine which is Christ, and so come to share his life, and are enlivened by his life sap coursing within. It is a powerful image of oneness, dependence, and aliveness. Fruitfulness is the result of this relationship. A term which John likes to use to express this is the verb to 'dwell', or 'abide', or 'remain in'. Jesus makes his home in us and we make ours in him (also 6:56). And there is a permanency about this remarkable mutuality, closeness and profound intimacy.

Earlier, in the block of material which John devotes to the Last Supper (ch.13-17), the close connection between washing and relationship with Jesus in his death and resurrection is highlighted in a dramatic and interesting way.

> *1* Now before the festival of the Passover, Jesus knew that his hour had come to depart from this world and go to the Father. Having loved his own who were in the world, he loved them to the end. *2* The devil had already put it into the heart of Judas son of Simon Iscariot to betray him. And during supper *3* Jesus, knowing that the Father had given all things into his hands, and that he had come from God and was going to God, *4* got up from the table, took off his outer robe, and tied a towel around himself. *5* Then he poured water into a basin and began to wash the disciples' feet and to wipe them with the towel that was tied around him. *6* He came to Simon Peter, who said to him, "Lord, are you going to wash my feet?" *7* Jesus answered, "You do not know now what I am doing, but later you will understand." *8* Peter said to him, "You will never wash my feet." Jesus answered, "Unless I wash you, you have no share with me." *9* Simon Peter said to him, "Lord, not my feet only but also my hands and my head!" *10* Jesus said to him, "One who has bathed does not need to wash, except for the feet, but is entirely clean. And you are clean, though not all of you." *11* For he knew who was to betray him; for this reason he said, "Not all of you are clean." *12* After he had washed their feet, had put on his robe, and had returned to the table, he said to them, "Do you know what I have done to you? *13* You call me Teacher and Lord – and you are right, for that is what I am. *14* So if I, your Lord and Teacher, have washed your feet, you also ought to wash one another's feet. *15* For I have set you an example, that you also should do as I have done to you." (John 13:1-15)

The opening verse of this passage is very solemn. It informs the reader that it is Passover time, a feast pregnant with theological significance. In the earlier ministry there have been references to the 'hour' of Jesus, an 'hour' which lay in the future (2:4; 7:30; 8:20). This is a technical term used to describe the period which embraces Jesus' departure and return to the Father through suffering and death, resurrection and ascension. That 'hour' has now come (11:55-57; 12:20-24, 27-33). What is to take place will be a demonstration of Jesus' love for his disciples, his love to the end and to the uttermost – the Greek phrase (*eis telos*) can mean both.

Jesus and his disciples are at table for what will be a farewell meal. The context of love and friendship is fractured by the presence of evil and the threat of betrayal. Carefully and purposefully Jesus rises from table, removes his outer garment, pours water into a basin and, as a servant, silently and humbly sets about washing the feet of his disciples and drying them with a towel. A dialogue ensues between Peter and Jesus. Peter, struggling to cope with role reversal, objects strongly, and continues to object after Jesus' assurance that he will understand fully at a later date, a comment found on previous occasions (2:22; 12:16, 23). Then Jesus insists that he wash Peter if he is to have a share in his heritage, and be part of his company, and benefit from his love. Peter still interprets Jesus' words and actions in a literal way, and, going to the opposite extreme, begs Jesus to wash him entirely. To this Jesus replies that the one who has bathed is clean all over, a verb which suggests total immersion; there is no need to wash twice. [11]

This washing, this act of service by Jesus, is symbolic. It is a prophetic action. It points to his coming humiliating death in response to the Father's saving will and in self-giving love for others. The verbs used for his laying aside and putting on his garments are the same as those used of the Good Shepherd who lays down his life and takes it up again (10:11, 15, 17,18). After the 'hour' is completed and the Spirit outpoured, the cleansing action of baptismal washing will plunge believers into the reality of Jesus, introduce them into a shared existence. Central to that new shared relationship and the acceptance of Jesus as Lord and Master is the following of his example. Disciples, members of the Christian community, are to wash one another's feet; they are to accept as the radical norm and pattern of their lives the love and self-giving of Jesus to the uttermost. This passage presupposes the ritual and practice of baptism within the Johannine community, but the emphasis rests on its meaning and implications, and on its link with the death of Jesus.

Membership of a Community

THE BAPTISMAL OUTPOURING OF THE SPIRIT, then, achieves a liberating transition from darkness, sinfulness and death. It establishes a relationship with the Father as God's children, and it unites us with the Risen Christ. The imagery of vine and branches also suggests the existence of a community, thus recalling the picture drawn by Peter in the extract from Acts which we examined earlier. We are baptised into a community, into the new people of God. This aspect of baptism is highlighted in the following quotation from Matthew's Gospel. (12)

> 16 Now the eleven disciples went to Galilee, to the mountain to which Jesus had directed them. 17 When they saw him, they worshiped him; but some doubted. 18 And Jesus came and said to them, "All authority in heaven and on earth has been given to me. 19 Go therefore and make disciples of all nations, baptising them in the name of the Father and of the Son and of the Holy Spirit, 20 and teaching them to obey everything that I have commanded you. And remember, I am with you always, to the end of the age." (Matthew 28:16-20)

This extract is Matthew's version of the encounter between the Risen Jesus and his disciples. This Evangelist follows the tradition which locates the experience in Galilee, as was indicated by the angel at the tomb (28:7), and then by Jesus to the women slightly later (28:10). The format is in keeping with the template for appearance narratives in the Gospels. (13) There is a situation of loss, absence, bereavement. Jesus appears suddenly and unexpectedly. At first there is doubt or hesitancy or failure to recognise him. Then there is the climactic moment of recognition. Finally, Jesus sends on mission. In Matthew's version the emphasis is placed strongly on this element of commissioning.

For Matthew, the effect and meaning of the resurrection/exaltation of Jesus is that he has received from the Father universal, total and eternal dominion and authority. He is the messianic king in power, the judge and ruler of the end time, invested with the dignity and authority which Judaism traditionally attributed to God. Consequently, with this authority the Risen Jesus sends the eleven apostles out on mission. However, whereas during the ministry his own mission was restricted to the Jews alone (10:5; 15:24), now in the new era introduced by his death and resurrection, Jesus sends them to all the nations of the world. The age of exclusiveness is over. The location of this episode, in Galilee of the Gentiles (4:15, quoting Isaiah 8:23-9:1), is significant. As Matthew indicated in his infancy narrative, Jesus is Son of Abraham (1:1), and brings to fulfilment the promise that in him all nations of the world would be blessed (Genesis 22:18LXX).

The purpose of this mission, expressed strongly in the imperative, is to make people into disciples. This is to be achieved by baptising them. Baptism is the initiation rite by which the Christian community separates itself and its members from any other community, especially the Jewish community. Instead of circumcision, it is baptism that gives them an identity as the new people of God. Only here is baptism said to have been instituted and commanded by Jesus. It is quite remarkable that the recommended baptismal formula is trinitarian. Elsewhere in the New Testament, as we have seen, baptism is performed *'in the name of Jesus'* (Acts 2:38; 8:16), or *'into Christ'* (Romans 6:3; Galations 3:7). It appears that the trinitarian formula arose in Matthew's church, and came to be used there by the eighties. This was the form which eventually prevailed, being accepted in Rome by 150 AD. Through baptism believers are plunged into the name and life of the Trinity, immersed in the bonds of family love binding the three persons and binding together the members of the community. It is interesting that there is no explicit mention of the forgiveness of sins.

There are implications for those living in the community of the baptised. They are to obey all that Jesus has taught. He, not Moses, is the authoritative interpreter of the will of God. His word rather than the Torah is paramount and normative. His new followers are to make their own the values, attitudes, outlook, and agenda of Jesus. Finally, Jesus promises his abiding and lasting presence with his community, sustaining, enabling, energising across the world and throughout the ages. Here Matthew recalls his statement early in the Gospel that Jesus is Emmanuel, God-with-us (1:23, quoting Isaiah 7:14).

A Style of Living

MATTHEW, LUKE AND JOHN

OBEDIENCE TO WHAT JESUS HAS TAUGHT is, for Matthew, integral to life as a baptised disciple. Key elements of Jesus' teaching are brought together in the sermon on the mount (Matthew 5:1-7:29), which serves as a blueprint for life in the growing Kingdom. The original words of Jesus threw down a radical challenge not only to individuals, but outlined a new way to be Israel, to be the people of God. [14]   For Matthew too the sermon provides a charter for being Church. In Acts, Luke describes how the newly converted Christians *'remained faithful to the teaching of the apostles'* (Acts 2:42). I shall discuss other aspects of their living in the next chapter. In John, life as branches of the vine makes demands, and entails observance of the commandment to love as Jesus loves (John 15:12,17). After washing the feet of his disciples at their final Supper together, Jesus, as we have seen, instructs them to make this act of self-giving and service the pattern of their lives. Later, when Judas has departed from the room, he adds his final injunction:

> I give you a new commandment: love one another: you must love one another just as I have loved you. It is by your love for one another that everyone will recognise you as my disciples (13: 34-35).

Our dwelling in him and his dwelling in us overflows and reaches out in a characteristic love for others, a love modelled on the quality of his own loving.

PAUL

PAUL INCLUDES INSTRUCTIONS ON LIFESTYLE in all his letters, often reflecting concrete situations of struggle and tension, as in 1 Corinthians. There is an interesting summary in Romans:

> *8* Owe no one anything, except to love one another; for the one who loves another has fulfilled the law. *9* The commandments, "You shall not commit adultery; You shall not murder; You shall not steal; You shall not covet;" and any other commandment are summed up in this word, "Love your neighbour as yourself." *10* Love does no wrong to a neighbour; therefore, love is the fulfilling of the law (Romans 13:8-10).

Paul makes his view clear that if we pay to one another the debt of love, we shall thereby do all that we need to do for them. Love is the key to our relationships with others. If we love, we shall not hurt or harm, and so will inevitably fulfil the commandments. Here Paul is in harmony with the Gospel emphasis on the centrality of love.

Other Pauline extracts link our way of behaving with the presence of the Spirit in the heart of the Christian. An excellent illustration is found in the following rather lengthy excerpt from the letter to the Galatians:

> *13* For you were called to freedom, brothers and sisters; only do not use your freedom as an opportunity for self-indulgence, but through love become slaves to one another. *14* For the whole law is summed up in a single commandment, "You shall love your neighbour as yourself." *15* If, however, you bite and devour one another, take care

that you are not consumed by one another. *16* Live by the Spirit, I say, and do not gratify the desires of the flesh. *17* For what the flesh desires is opposed to the Spirit, and what the Spirit desires is opposed to the flesh; for these are opposed to each other, to prevent you from doing what you want.

18 But if you are led by the Spirit, you are not subject to the law. *19* Now the works of the flesh are obvious: fornication, impurity, licentiousness, *20* idolatry, sorcery, enmities, strife, jealousy, anger, quarrels, dissensions, factions, *21* envy, drunkenness, carousing, and things like these. I am warning you, as I warned you before: those who do such things will not inherit the kingdom of God. *22* By contrast, the fruit of the Spirit is love, joy, peace, patience, kindness, generosity, faithfulness, *23* gentleness, and self-control. There is no law against such things. *24* And those who belong to Christ Jesus have crucified the flesh with its passions and desires. *25* If we live by the Spirit, let us also be guided by the Spirit. *26* Let us not become conceited, competing against one another, envying one another (Galatians 5:13-26).

The Christian community is called to freedom, freedom from the Mosaic Law and freedom also from our selfish and sinful inclinations, the 'flesh'. But the freedom which the Spirit bestows, our new life in the Spirit, paradoxically leads the believer to embrace a new form of slavery, the slavery of self-giving love and service towards others. The community is called to live by the Spirit, be led by the Spirit, and this comes to expression in a distinctive life style, a characteristic ethos. This contrasts with the way of the flesh, the way of darkness, a negative pattern of behaviour, for Spirit and flesh are in opposition. Paul provides a representative list of types of 'flesh'-induced behaviour. Such catalogues of vices with their corresponding virtues are quite conventional, and elsewhere Paul offers other examples (see Romans 1:29-31; 1 Corinthians 5:10-11; 6:9-10; 2 Corinthians 12:20; 2 Timothy 3:2-5). This list, however, seems to be particularly applicable to the situation of the local Galatian church, for most of the actions itemised militate against concord and unity in the community.

The indwelling and energising Spirit, on the other hand, bears fruit of a different order, inner qualities and characteristics which spontaneously overflow into action which upbuilds the community. (15) We belong to Christ Jesus; we are in Christ. The destructive inclinations once crucified with Christ in baptism do return to assail us, but they need not control us. There is still sin in the Christian life and the Christian community, but it need not reign, for the Spirit provides the power to overcome sin. So we seek to live by the Spirit, walk in step with the Spirit, allow the Spirit to influence and guide every aspect and dimension of our living, transforming us from within.

The Image of the Seal

THERE IS ANOTHER SCRIPTURAL IMAGE which draws together several of the themes which we have been considering. It is the symbol of the 'seal' as a sign of belonging and of consecration. Used of Jesus by John (6:27; 10:36), it is used of the Christian by Paul in 2 Corinthians 1:22 and is found also in Ephesians 1:13 and 4:30.

> 21 But it is God who establishes us with you in Christ and has anointed us, 22 by putting his seal on us and giving us his Spirit in our hearts as a first instalment (2 Corinthians 1:21-22).

In context these verses form part of Paul's defence against criticism by the Corinthians for his failure to keep his promise of a further visit. (16)   He seeks to base his own trustworthiness on their common Christian experience, their common rootedness in Christ which God has achieved. Anointing, sealing, and the giving of the Spirit reflect the one fundamental conversion event celebrated in baptism. The commercial and legal term 'seal' now refers to baptism as a sign that we belong to God's people, are claimed as God's property, genuinely identifiable and secure as God's possession. The presence of the Spirit in our hearts is like a first instalment or deposit which guarantees full payment later, when God brings his promises to fulfilment.

Similar ideas are found in the letter to the Ephesians:

> *13* In him you also, when you had heard the word of truth, the gospel of your salvation, and had believed in him, were marked with the seal of the promised Holy Spirit; *14* this is the pledge of our inheritance toward redemption as God's own people, to the praise of his glory (Ephesians 1:13-14).

This quotation is taken from the hymn with which the letter opens, and which celebrates God's plan of salvation. God is praised for his loving decision to make us adopted children in Christ, giving us freedom and forgiveness through his blood. God's overarching plan is to bring everything together in Christ, and the Gentiles too are caught up in this gracious purpose. The process or route consists in listening to the proclamation of the Good News, the apostolic preaching of the message of salvation, and putting trust in it, believing. It is through the gift of the Spirit in baptism that we are drawn into the saving life of God and become God's children.

There are two points to note here. Firstly, the reception of the gift of the Spirit is described as being *'marked with the seal'*. In the Old Testament the seal, a mark on the forehead, was a sign of election, belonging, protection (Ezekiel 9:4). Here the Holy Spirit is the seal, the sign which characterises our Christian existence, the indication that we belong to God, that we share the salvation gained through Christ, that we become members of the new People of God. Secondly, the Spirit alive within us is understood as the guarantee of the full inheritance which we shall come to possess by God's gift at the end of time, when God's plan is fully accomplished and salvation completely achieved. In the meantime there is a kind of tension between the 'now' and the 'not yet', what we are and what we will become. But the Spirit guarantees continuity and fulfilment.

This future fulfilment of our redemption and liberation is emphasised in the second quotation from this letter:

> *30* And do not grieve the Holy Spirit of God, with which you were marked with a seal for the day of redemption (Ephesians 4:30).

Again it is the Spirit with which we were 'sealed' in baptism who is our guarantee as we look to our ultimate future. This quotation is found in a very different context in the letter. After an exhortation that the community, bonded by the Spirit, should live in unity, and so reach maturity in Christ, the implications of living this newly acquired life 'in Christ', of having 'put on' Christ are spelled out. Expressions of the former self, the old way of living, must be avoided, such as lies, anger, theft, foul language, bitterness, shouting. Such behaviour is said to *grieve the Holy Spirit*' (see Isaiah 63:10; 1 Thessalonians 4:8), because it is destructive of community, and not in keeping with that unity in Christ which we are called to manifest through our humility, gentleness and patience (4:2), our generosity, sympathy and forgiveness (4:32).

Conclusion

In this chapter we have considered different strands of the rich texture offered by the scriptural presentation of baptism.

CHILDREN OF GOD

THROUGH THE GIFT OF THE SPIRIT which is bestowed in connection with the water rite our sins are forgiven and we are drawn into the life of God, becoming God's children, able to call God 'Abba', Father. We are also made one with Christ in his death and resurrection. There is a new dimension to our human personhood, to our identity. Part of life's challenge is to allow the awareness of our identity to penetrate our mind and heart, to permeate our life. God loves me. I share God's life. I am always in the heart of God. I belong to God. Nothing is ordinary, routine or prosaic any more, for it is caught up in God's loving presence. I am always on 'holy ground'. Awareness of who I have become through baptism can make an enormous difference to the way I view and accept myself, relate to others, comprehend life's meaning. Such transforming awareness can be deepened by reflective prayer, by listening to God's love, that love spoken most clearly in Jesus, the Word enfleshed.

IN CHRIST

JESUS IS OUR BROTHER AND FRIEND, who walks our way with us, and draws us into the mystery of his dying and rising. Through baptism we are made one with him, like limbs on the body, branches on the vine. Another aspect of life's challenge is that we grow in his likeness, come to share his outlook, attitudes and values, allow the Spirit to fashion our hearts so that they resemble his in his surrendering and trusting love for the Father, his self-forgetfulness and self-giving love for others. We need to make space for him, spend time with him in prayer, reflect on the scriptures, allow them to impact on our life, to enlighten and challenge our experience. We need to discern what it is that love is asking of us and what faithfulness to him entails in our very different world.

MEMBERS OF GOD'S PEOPLE

BAPTISM ALSO DRAWS US INTO THE COMMUNION/community of the new people of God. Through the Spirit we are bonded with others in the depths of our being beyond differences and distinctions. We form one body. A major challenge is to break out of religious individualism and embrace the communal aspect of our identity, developing our sense of relatedness, belonging, shared existence. A further challenge is to make this oneness visible, to translate it into action, to foster unity, to strive to overcome division. This topic we shall pursue later in connection with the eucharist. We are all gifted in so many ways. We are invited to use our gifts in the service of our community and its mission. In today's Church more opportunities for this are becoming available, a development to be encouraged. Such active participation is a natural expression of our baptismal consecration.

Our coming to share the life of God is a free gift, an immense surprise, beyond our wildest dreams and our natural capabilities. To live this relationship with integrity and gratitude demands a certain outlook and lifestyle, an ongoing process of conversion and growth, following the revelation and teaching of Jesus. We need to support one another in this ongoing endeavour. But, as in the case of Jesus, relationship implies mission. Through our baptism we are caught up into the mission of Jesus; we are sent out into the community and into the world. This important and exciting theme will form part of our reflection on the sacrament of confirmation.

A brief quotation from the letter to Titus provides a closing summary:

> 4 But when the goodness and loving kindness of God our Saviour appeared, 5 he saved us, not because of any works of righteousness that we had done, but according to his mercy, through the water of rebirth and renewal by the Holy Spirit. 6 This Spirit he poured out on us richly through Jesus Christ our Saviour, 7 so that, having been justified by his grace, we might become heirs according to the hope of eternal life (Titus 3:4-7).

NOTES

(1) See R.E. Brown, *A Once-and-Coming Spirit at Pentecost* (Collegeville, Liturgical Press 1994), p.11-19. Useful commentaries on Acts include: J. Crowe, *Acts* (Dublin, Veritas 1979); J.A. Fitzmyer, *The Acts of the Apostles* (Doubleday, London 1998); E. Haenchen, *The Acts of the Apostles* (Oxford, Blackwell 1992); L.T. Johnson, *The Acts of the Apostles* (Collegeville, Liturgical Press 1992); J. Munck, *Acts* (New York, Doubleday 1967). On the New Testament in general, see R.E. Brown, *An Introduction to the New Testament* (London, Doubleday 1997); E. Charpentier, *How to Read the New Testament* (London, SCM 1982).

(2) See N.T. Wright, *The Challenge of Jesus* (London, SPCK 2000), p.48; *Jesus and the Victory of God* (London, SPCK 1996), p.268-274.

(3) I have found the following commentaries on Mark's Gospel helpful: H. Anderson, *The Gospel of Mark* (London, Oliphants 1976); W. Harrington, *Mark* (Dublin, Veritas 1979); M.D. Hooker, *The Gospel according to St. Mark* (London, A&C Black 1991); D. McBride, *The Gospel of Mark* (Dublin, Dominican Publications 1996); F.J. Moloney, *The Gospel of Mark. A Commentary* (Peabody, Hendrickson Publishers 2002); D.E. Nineham, *St. Mark* (London, Penguin Books 1963).

(4) See J.P. Meier, *A Marginal Jew* (London, Doubleday 1994), vol.2, p.19-233.

(5) In Matthew John the Baptist hesitates and Jesus insists. Luke mentions the baptism in passing, without emphasis. John, though clearly aware of the tradition, does not mention the baptism explicitly. Perhaps they felt uncomfortable with the concept of a sinless Jesus submitting to a baptism of repentance, and considered it inappropriate that Jesus should receive baptism from someone inferior.

(6) Useful commentaries include: F.F. Bruce, *The Epistle to the Galatians* (Exeter, Paternoster 1982); C. Osick, *Galatians* (Dublin, Veritas 1980); B. Witherington III, *Grace in Galatia* (Edinburgh, T&T Clark 1998); E.H. Maly, *Romans* (Dublin, Veritas 1979).

(7) F.F. Bruce, *Galatians*, p.199.

(8) In my treatment of extracts from the Fourth Gospel I am particularly indebted to the following: C.K. Barrett, *The Gospel according to John* (London, SPCK 1978); T.L. Brodie, *The Gospel according to John* (Oxford, OUP 1993); R.E. Brown, *The Gospel according to John* (London, Chapmans 1972), 2 vols.; R.A. Culpepper *Anatomy of the Fourth Gospel* (Philadelphia, Fortress 1983); C.H. Dodd, *The Interpretation of the Fourth Gospel* (Cambridge, CUP 1968); B. Lindars, *The Gospel of John* (London, Oliphants 1972); F.J. Moloney, *The Gospel of John* (Collegeville, Liturgical Press 1998); R. Schnackenburg, *The Gospel of John* (London, B&O vol.1 1968, vol.2 1980, vol.3 1982); M.W.G. Stibbe, *John. Readings* (Sheffield, JSOT Press 1993).

(9) *Amen* was commonly used in Hebrew after a wish or prayer, meaning 'so be it', or to affirm and express agreement with something said by another. It seems to have been a characteristic of Jesus to use it frequently at the beginning of a saying in order to add emphasis, solemnly guaranteeing the truth of what he is about to say. This usage is not found in Jewish literature or in the New Testament outside the Gospels. The Fourth

Evangelist tends to double the *Amen*. See J. Jeremias, *The Prayers of Jesus* (London, SCM 1967), p.112-115.

(10) Helpful commentaries on Ephesians are: R. Schnackenburg, *The Epistle to the Ephesians* (Edinburg, T&T Clark 1991); L. Swain, *Ephesians* (Dublin, Veritas 1980).

(11) Some manuscripts add 'except for the feet' in v.10, and the NRSV translation, which we are using in this book, follows these. Other manuscripts omit the phrase, as can be seen in the REB and NJB translations. Many scholars hold that the latter group of manuscripts is more likely to reflect the original, and believe that early copyists added the phrase in order to solve the problem of the forgiveness of sin after baptism.

(12) On Matthew I have found the following helpful: F.W. Beare, *The Gospel according to Matthew* (Oxford, Blackwell 1981); W.D. Davis and D.C. Allison, *A Critical and Exegetical Commentary on the Gospel according to Saint Matthew* (Edinburgh, T&T Clark 1988); C.S. Keener, *A Commentary on the Gospel of Matthew* (Grand Rapids, Eerdmans 1999); J.P. Meier, *Matthew* (Dublin, Veritas 1980); F.J. Moloney, *This is the Gospel of the Lord (Year A)* (Homebush, St. Paul 1992); D. Senior, *Matthew* (Nashville, Abingdon Press 1998).

(13) See R.E. Brown, *John*, p.972-975; also useful is his *A Risen Christ in Eastertime* (Collegeville, Liturgical Press 1991); D. Catchpole, *Resurrection People* (London, DLT 2000); N. Perrin, *The Resurrection Narratives: A New Approach* (London, SCM 1977). The Gospels offer a variety of narratives describing the encounter between the Risen Jesus and the disciples. Some take place in Galilee (Matthew, John 21 and (implicitly) Mark); others in Jerusalem (Luke, John 20). The Jerusalem and Galilee traditions do not harmonise easily. Many scholars maintain that the Evangelists are narrating the same basic appearance to the eleven in which the Church was founded and commissioned. A view commonly held suggests that historically the disciples left Jerusalem in disillusionment and fear and returned to Galilee. There Jesus appeared to Peter and resurrection faith was born. He gathered the others and the main appearance took place, with the giving of the Spirit and the commissioning. Subsequently they returned to Jerusalem for the feast of Pentecost, where the charismatic outpouring of the Spirit took place and they initiated the Christian mission.

(14) See N.T. Wright, *Challenge*, p.27-28.

(15) The fruits of the Spirit listed in verses 22-23 are often linked today with the sacrament of confirmation.

(16) See F.F. Bruce, *1 & 2 Corinthians* (London, Oliphants 1971); F.T. Fallon, *2 Corinthians* (Dublin, Veritas 1980); L. Kreitzer, *2 Corinthians* (Sheffield, Sheffield Academic Press 1996); J. Murphy-O'Connor, *The Theology of the Second Letter to the Corinthians* (Cambridge, CUP 1991); N. Watson, *The Second Epistle to the Corinthians* (London, Epworth 1993); Ben Witherington III, *Conflict and Community in Corinth* (Michigan, Eerdmans 1995).

CHAPTER TWO

Confirmation

IN THE LAST CHAPTER we reflected on a
selection of scriptural texts which, I believe,
underpin and clarify our understanding of the
sacrament of baptism. In this chapter we turn to
the sacrament of confirmation, recalling the
proviso that from the scriptural point of view
the distinction between the two is tenuous.
There is in the New Testament no mention of
confirmation as a rite separate from baptism.[1]
The Holy Spirit is obviously very much at the
centre of both sacraments. We shall concentrate
on images of the Spirit, the Spirit's empowering
the Christian for mission, and different ways in
which that mission is articulated. We shall
examine texts referring to the Paraclete, and
finally, we shall consider Pentecost and its
aftermath according to Acts.

Images of the Spirit

TWO IMAGES WHICH ARE FOUND IN SCRIPTURE for the Spirit of God
are wind/breath and water. They occur both in the Old Testament
and the New, and open up some rich insights. I propose to concentrate mainly on Genesis, Ezekiel and John.

GENESIS

WE FIRST ENCOUNTER THESE IMAGES in the book of Genesis, right at the dawn of things, the surprise of creation. [2]

> *1* In the beginning God created heaven and earth. *2* Now the earth was a formless void, there was darkness over the deep, with a divine wind sweeping over the waters (Genesis 1:1-2 NJB).

The twofold creation story is a fascinating expression of religious poetry. In this first version, normally attributed to the priestly tradition, it is the view of many scholars that verse one provides a summary, which is subsequently spelled out in detail (Genesis 1:2-2:4). The sovereign God freely and effortlessly brings everything into existence. It is not absolutely clear whether the writer envisages creation from nothing, or the organisation of already existing chaos. The primeval chaos is described in terms of primordial darkness, deep waters, and an awesome, mighty wind. This last phrase can be translated as 'divine wind', or a 'wind from God', or 'the spirit of God'. The NEB reads: *'and the spirit of God hovered over the surface of the water'*. The image of wind vividly and concretely conveys a sense of God's powerful, energetic presence moving in a mysterious way over the face of the deep, eager to transform and to introduce life and shape, order and beauty.

The second version, found in the Yahwist tradition, is very different, but contains the same two images.

> *4* At the time when Yahweh God made earth and heaven *5* there was as yet no wild bush on the earth nor had any wild plant yet sprung up, for Yahweh God had not sent rain on the earth, nor was there any man to till the soil. *6* Instead, water flowed out of the ground, and watered all the surface of the soil. *7* Yahweh shaped man from the soil of the ground, and blew the breath of life into his nostrils, and the man became a living being (Genesis 2:4-7 NJB).

Here it is man who is created first. Prior to this there is a desolate picture of a barren, infertile land, watered by a rising mist or a flood surging from beneath. The creation of man, the central event, takes place in two stages. First of all, God takes clods of earth, and like a skilful potter moulds and shapes it into a human form. In the Hebrew there is a play on the words for earth (*adamah*) and man (*adam*), which brings out the close bond between man and the soil. Then God breathes life into this inanimate, material body, and man becomes a living person, a human being. The intensely personal imagery highlights the dependency and close intimacy of man's relationship with God. Man is indeed made in the *'image and likeness of God'* (Genesis 1:26), his aliveness is the gift of God. As Job puts it: *'God's was the spirit that made me, Shaddai's the breath that gave me life'* (33:4).

The sense of life's giftedness and fragility is found too in the Psalms:

> 29 Turn away your face and they panic; take back your breath and they die
> and revert to dust.
> 30 Send out your breath and life begins;
> you renew the face of the earth (Psalm 104:29-30 NJB).

EZEKIEL

ONE OF MY FAVOURITE OLD TESTAMENT PASSAGES is the dramatic scene in Ezekiel 37. (3) The prophet is taken into the valley of the dead, a scene of enormous desolation. Vast quantities of dry bones litter the valley bottom. The prophet is ordered by Yahweh to prophesy, and at his word the bones come clattering together to form skeletons, and are covered with sinews and flesh and skin. There then occurs a pause in the narration, which delays the climax, as the reader is informed that as yet there was no life in them. The prophet then proceeds:

9 Then he said to me, "Prophesy to the breath, prophesy, mortal, and say to the breath: Thus says the Lord God: Come from the four winds, O breath, and breathe upon these slain, that they may live." 10 I prophesied as he commanded me, and the breath came into them, and they lived, and stood on their feet, a vast multitude (Ezekiel 37:9-10).

The interpretation follows. The bones are the house of exiled Israel, a people riven with despair, their spirits broken. The imagery then changes slightly, as Yahweh promises reversal and restoration.

12 Therefore prophesy, and say to them, Thus says the Lord God: I am going to open your graves, and bring you up from your graves, O my people; and I will bring you back to the land of Israel. 13 And you shall know that I am the Lord, when I open your graves, and bring you up from your graves, O my people. 14 I will put my spirit within you, and you shall live, and I will place you on your own soil; then you shall know that I, the Lord, have spoken and will act, says the Lord."

This passage provides such a vivid and dramatic double imaging of God's merciful and transforming power in freely calling the house of Israel back to life. This is a corporate event. It is the restoring of a people, the enlivening of a nation. The language and the images of wind and life-breath recall the Genesis story. The breath which gives life is the spirit of God.

In the previous chapter the prophet Ezekiel also explores the symbolic potential of water and spirit.

24 I will take you from the nations, and gather you from all the countries, and bring you into your own land. 25 I will sprinkle clean water upon you, and you shall be clean from all your uncleannesses, and from all your idols I will cleanse you. 26 A new heart I will give you, and a new spirit I will

> put within you; and I will remove from your body the heart
> of stone and give you a heart of flesh. *27* I will put my spirit
> within you, and make you follow my statutes and be careful
> to observe my ordinances. *28* Then you shall live in the land
> that I gave to your ancestors; and you shall be my people,
> and I will be your God (Ezekiel 36:24-28).

The people are in exile as a result of their evil behaviour. They have
shed much blood and have offered worship to idols, and their hearts
have become hardened to Yahweh, like stone. Yahweh resolves to
vindicate his name, and through the prophet promises to bring them
home. God will cleanse them of their defilement through the sprin-
kling of water. Then God will bestow the gift of a new heart and
spirit to replace their hearts of stone. This creative intervention of
God will remove their obduracy, and God's spirit within them will
bring about an inner transformation, enabling them to shape their
lives in accordance with his commandments and will, so that they
will indeed live as God's people. Thus, in the form of a promise,
Ezekiel anticipates what the new Testament makes the basis of the
inner life of the Christian. (4)

JOHN

IT IS TO THE NEW TESTAMENT THAT WE NOW TURN. Here it is the
Fourth Evangelist who has taken this imagery of wind and water and
exploited it most effectively as a vehicle for communicating the
Good News about what is offered us through the person and mission
of Jesus. (5)

In the last chapter we reflected on the passage featuring Nicodemus,
in which the link is made between water and spirit. The extract
which I wish to examine this time is a continuation of that reading.

> *5* Jesus answered, "Very truly, I tell you, no one can enter
> the kingdom of God without being born of water and

Spirit. *6* What is born of the flesh is flesh, and what is born of the Spirit is spirit.

8 The wind blows where it chooses, and you hear the sound of it, but you do not know where it comes from or where it goes. So it is with everyone who is born of the Spirit." (John 3:5-6, 8)

You will recall John's two-tier universe, the above/below, heavenly/earthly, Spirit/flesh. The gap between the tiers is bridged only through the gift of God in sending His Son. This makes another birth possible, a new birth by water and Spirit through which we enter the Kingdom of God, or are saved, or come already to share 'eternal life', the very life of God.

The second image, found in verse 8, plays on the rich meaning of the Greek word which can indicate the wind, breath, and Spirit. Although the wind is part of our common human experience and we frequently witness its effects, there is something inexplicable and unpredictable about it, something mysterious about its coming and going, something which cannot be controlled. Anyone with fell-walking experience will be familiar with this. Jesus tells Nicodemus that the Spirit too cannot be controlled or understood. People born of this Spirit have their origin and destiny in the mystery of God, and the effects of the Spirit's presence are manifest in their lives.

In the following chapter John narrates the fascinating encounter between Jesus and the woman from Samaria.

> *4* But he had to go through Samaria. *5* So he came to a Samaritan city called Sychar, near the plot of ground that Jacob had given to his son Joseph. *6* Jacob's well was there, and Jesus, tired out by his journey, was sitting by the well. It was about noon. *7* A Samaritan woman came to draw water, and Jesus said to her, "Give me a drink." *8* (His disciples had gone to the city to buy food.) *9* The Samaritan woman said to him, "How is it that you, a Jew, ask a drink

of me, a woman of Samaria?" (Jews do not share things in
common with Samaritans.) *10* Jesus answered her, "If you
knew the gift of God, and who it is that is saying to you,
'Give me a drink,' you would have asked him, and he
would have given you living water." *11* The woman said to
him, "Sir, you have no bucket, and the well is deep. Where
do you get that living water? *12* Are you greater than our
ancestor Jacob, who gave us the well, and with his sons and
his flocks drank from it?" *13* Jesus said to her, "Everyone
who drinks of this water will be thirsty again,
14 but those who drink of the water that I will give them will
never be thirsty. The water that I will give will become in
them a spring of water gushing up to eternal life."
(John 4:4-14)

This is a beautiful passage. Tired and thirsty from his journey, Jesus
flouts convention and asks the woman for a drink. The disciples have
(conveniently) gone shopping *en masse*. When the woman
registers surprise at such a request on the lips of a Jew, Jesus speaks
of 'the gift of God', and 'who it is' that has entered into conversation
with her (his identity), two of the main themes of the story. The term
'living water' is another phrase with double meaning. It can refer to
fresh, spring water, in contrast to flat cistern or pond water.
The woman takes this meaning, and speaks about practical things
like wells and buckets. She goes on to defend her 'patch' and her
local tradition about the great patriarch Jacob. There is much irony in
her question whether Jesus is greater than Jacob! But 'living water' is
water of a qualitatively different kind. It is water which slakes thirst
permanently, and which touches the depths of the human spirit.
This water will be like an inner spring, a fountain within, gushing up
abundantly and inexhaustibly, an ongoing source of 'eternal life'.

There is much scholarly discussion about the meaning of 'living
water'. Many think that its prime meaning is the revelation which
Jesus brings. Others maintain that it also refers to the Holy Spirit or
life mediated by the Spirit. I prefer the both/and approach! The link

with the Nicodemus passage, the other references to baptism (3:22-27; 4:1-2), and the reference to the Spirit which now follows, suggest to me that a reference to the Spirit should be admitted.

The discussion between Jesus and the woman continues. After Jesus has given her a shock by revealing that he knows a great deal about her rather shady past life, the topic changes to another divisive issue, the nature and place of true worship. Jesus says to her:

> 23 But the hour is coming, and is now here, when the true worshippers will worship the Father in spirit and truth, for the Father seeks such as these to worship him. 24 God is spirit, and those who worship him must worship in spirit and truth.

There is no point in perpetuating the long-standing controversy about the relative merits of the Jerusalem Temple or the Samaritan Temple at Gerizim as centres of worship. A new era is being inaugurated, and with it a new style of worship which supersedes both places. This new worship will take place in the Spirit of truth. God will be worshipped as Father by those to whom the Spirit has been given, those 'born again', who have become God's children. This possibility of new worship comes as a gift. Human beings are empowered to worship in this new way as a result of the Father's seeking and the gift of the Spirit.

The next extract which contains this theme comes from a section of the Fourth Gospel which deals with the Jewish feast of Tabernacles. [6] This feast was a celebration of light and water. Against the background of the Temple brightly illuminated at night, Jesus claims to be the true light of the world. Against the background of processions and ceremonies connected with water and harvest, he speaks of himself as the solution to the deepest thirsts of our human heart. Jesus fulfils and transcends the meaning of the Jewish feast.

The feast lasted a whole week. On the final day Jesus stands in public and cries out aloud:

> 37 "Let anyone who is thirsty come to me! 38 Let anyone who believes in me come and drink! As scripture says, 'From his heart shall flow streams of living water.' "
> 39 He was speaking of the Spirit which those who believed in him were to receive; for there was no Spirit as yet because Jesus was not yet glorified (John 7:37-39 NJB).

There are several points of interest in these verses. Firstly, we again find the image of 'living water', life-giving water. Here its significance is rendered explicit by the narrator's comment. It refers to the Spirit. Secondly, because the Greek text is a little ambiguous, there is a debate amongst scholars concerning the source of this 'living water'. Some take it that the source is Jesus. It is from his heart that the living waters flow. It is he who provides the drink (as in 4:14). He is the 'bread of life' in chapter six, and the Good Shepherd in chapter ten. In the course of the Gospel he replaces the Sabbath, the Passover, the feast of Dedication. This view is called the Christological interpretation. Other commentators suggest that the waters flow from the heart of the believer; through being joined with Christ there is a sense in which the Christian becomes a life-giving source. The NRSV adopts this interpretation in its text: *As the scripture has said, 'Out of the believer's heart shall flow rivers of living water.'*

Thirdly, the passage of scripture referred to here may be Ezekiel 47:1-11, which speaks of ever-deepening water flowing from the Temple, bringing wholesomeness and abundant life wherever it flows. Or the passage could be Zechariah 14:8, which describes living waters flowing from Jerusalem in both summer and winter, and heading east and west. Fourthly, an explicit link is made between the giving of the Spirit and the glorification of Jesus, and you will recall what was said in the last chapter about the 'lifting up' of Jesus. It is precisely when his 'hour' has come and he has been 'lifted up' that the Spirit and the new life the Spirit brings become available to the believer.

It is to this event that we now turn.

> 28 After this, when Jesus knew that all was now finished, he
> said (in order to fulfil the scripture), "I am thirsty." 29 A jar
> full of sour wine was standing there. So they put a sponge
> full of the wine on a branch of hyssop and held it to his
> mouth. 30 When Jesus had received the wine, he said, "It is
> finished." Then he bowed his head and gave up his spirit
> (John 19:28-30).

This is a theologically rich passage, and again there are several interesting points to be considered. (7) Firstly, whilst Jesus' thirst is
doubtless factual and easy to understand in the situation, it probably
also carries a symbolic significance. It may refer to his longing to return
to the Father, or his intention to drink the cup of suffering which he
mentioned in the garden (18:11). It could indicate his desire that we be
saved. Some scholars, however, believe that what is intended here is
that Jesus thirsts, now that his hour has come, to give the Spirit. There
are two arguments used in favour of this view. The first is structural:

Jesus	aware that all is finished
	said: 'I thirst'
Others	the vinegar incident
Jesus	said: 'It is finished'
	handed over the Spirit

The word of Jesus about thirst and the handing over of the Spirit are
structurally in parallel, suggesting that they go together. They thus
balance the parallelism between Jesus' awareness that all is completed and his final assertion that this is so. The other argument stems
from the presence once again of misunderstanding. Jesus speaks
about his thirst. The soldiers take him literally and respond by offering him a drink. Jesus indicates his real meaning by bowing his head
and handing over the Spirit. The same pattern may operate here as in
the incident discussed earlier when Jesus acknowledges his thirst by
asking the Samaritan woman for a drink, and then the roles are
reversed and Jesus becomes the provider of 'living water'.

A second significant point is the phrase with which John describes Jesus' death: *'he handed over the spirit'*. At one level it means 'he breathed his last', 'he breathed out his life'; 'he died'. In the overall context of the Gospel, where we have already seen John using the various meanings of the word for breath and wind and spirit, the deeper significance of the term suggests that Jesus completes his task by bowing towards his mother and the beloved disciple at the foot of the cross and handing over to them the Holy Spirit. They are representative believers, the nucleus of the new covenant community, the new people of God, the Church. Now that he is uplifted and glorified, he can bestow the Spirit.

Thirdly, the flow of water, recalling the water gushing from the rock in Exodus (Exodus 17:16; Numbers 20:11), is the climax of the theme of water which has coursed through the narrative, and fulfils the words of Jesus in 7:37-39. The living water pouring forth from within the uplifted Jesus is the symbol of the gift of the Spirit. There is a line of continuity between the thirst, the breathing of the Spirit and the water flow.

Fourthly, the final words of Jesus: *'It is finished'* ring out as a cry of victory, signifying 'mission accomplished'. You will recall that in the last chapter, when examining the account of Jesus' baptism, I referred to the idea that through the Spirit Jesus is anointed for mission, and that mission is a central element of our Christian baptism. I said then that I would develop that idea in this chapter. In John's Gospel one of the hallmarks of Jesus is his sense of mission and his commitment to fulfilling it. More than forty times Jesus articulates his conviction of 'being sent', or, equivalently, 'having come'. We find on his lips expressions like these:

> Jesus said to them, "My food is to do the will of him who sent me and to complete his work." (4:34)

> "...for I have come down from heaven, not to do my own will, but the will of him who sent me." (6:38)
> "But I have a testimony greater than John's. The works that

the Father has given me to complete, the very works that I am doing, testify on my behalf that the Father has sent me." (5:36)

"I glorified you on earth by finishing the work that you gave me to do." (17:4)

And so the last words of the earthly Jesus refer to the completion of the task given to him by the Father, the fulfilment of his mission. For the Fourth Evangelist, no less than Mark whom we considered in chapter one, Jesus is totally referred to the Father, and totally taken up with mission. Relationship and mission go together, like the two faces of the one coin.

In the last chapter we discussed the resurrection narrative in Matthew, which concludes with the great commission, a commissioning explicitly including baptism and the making of disciples. The main resurrection appearance in John has a very different setting. It takes place on the evening of Easter Day in Jerusalem.

> *19* When it was evening on that day, the first day of the week, and the doors of the house where the disciples had met were locked for fear of the Jews, Jesus came and stood among them and said, "Peace be with you." *20* After he said this, he showed them his hands and his side. Then the disciples rejoiced when they saw the Lord. *21* Jesus said to them again, "Peace be with you. As the Father has sent me, so I send you." *22* When he had said this, he breathed on them and said to them, "Receive the Holy Spirit. *23* If you forgive the sins of any, they are forgiven them; if you retain the sins of any, they are retained." (20:19-23)

Elements of the basic literary pattern or template are clearly present: the bereft situation, with an emphasis on the disciples' fear, barricaded behind closed doors. Jesus suddenly and unexpectedly appears, and stands among them. The element of doubt is omitted, because John develops that aspect by personifying the theme in Thomas, and there is a separate narrative to deal with it (20: 24-29). The disciples recognise Jesus and are filled with joy. Finally, there is the commissioning. Here John's wording is particularly significant:

As the Father sent me, so I am sending you.

The Father's sending of Jesus, such a fundamental datum of the narrative, is the model for Jesus' sending his disciples. We are caught up in his mission, and into his relationship with the Father. To empower the disciples for mission, the Risen Jesus *'breathed on them'*, (again the image of breath and wind) and said: *'Receive the Holy Spirit'*. It is really now that the mission of Jesus is completed. Through being 'lifted up' in cross death and resurrection, he has returned to the Father and can now bestow the gift of the Spirit (anticipated on Calvary), which makes it possible for us to become children of God, newly born, gifted with a new dimension of aliveness called 'eternal life'. It is now that the relationship with the Father and with Jesus, which we considered in the previous chapter, becomes possible, as also membership of the new covenant community, and participation in mission to the world.

The images of water and wind/breath are woven like a fascinating and rich thread throughout the Gospel of John, developing and deepening their use in the Old Testament. The Spirit creates and sustains, gives life, creates children of God, enables true worship, forms a people, empowers for mission.

Mission

THE THEME OF MISSION has occurred several times in our reflections so far. It is central to our understanding of Jesus, and is fundamental to our conception of Christian living. In the Gospels the theme is articulated in a number of complementary ways. I find it helpful to consider these as models or paradigms of mission.

TO GIVE LIGHT AND LIFE

SINCE IN THE LAST FEW PAGES we have been concentrating on the Fourth Gospel, we can launch our exploration there. One of the ways in which John portrays the mission of Jesus is through the imagery of light and life. Jesus comes in order to be the light of the world, the unique and authoritative revealer of the Father, and he is sent to give life to the world, life in all its fullness (10:10).

Much of John's rich symbolism suggests this revelation motif. In the context of the feast of Tabernacles, when the city at night was bathed in candle light, Jesus claims that it is he who is the light of the world (8:12). The subsequent healing of the man born blind and his journey into the vision of faith illustrate the truth and significance of this claim (9:1-38). In the dialogue with the Samaritan woman he offers living water, which is often interpreted as meaning revelation and teaching, as well as referring to the Spirit (4:10). Jesus is the bread of life, which in the earlier part of the famous discourse is generally thought to refer primarily to revelation (6:25-51). In the Supper Discourse he calls his disciples friends because he has disclosed to them everything he has learned from the Father (15:15). At the conclusion of his final prayer Jesus claims to have revealed to 'his own' the Father's name, the very being of God (17:26). He is able to make God known because he has come from God, remains close to the Father's heart (1:18), and is taught by the Father (8:26,40).

When speaking to Nicodemus Jesus, as we have seen, explains that God in his love has sent him into the world so that believers may have eternal life (3:16-17). In elucidating his claim to be the Good Shepherd he states that he has come so that the sheep *'may have life and have it to the full'* (10:10). This aspect of his mission is illustrated by three signs: the cure of the centurion's son (4:46f), the healing of the cripple by the Bethesda pool (5:1f), and especially by the raising of Lazarus (11:1f). Jesus is, in fact, the resurrection and the life (11:25).

As Jesus was sent by the Father, so we his disciples are sent, empowered by the Spirit (20:21) to witness to, reveal and make known the love of God, which is the truth that sets people free (8:32). We do this through our words; we communicate it especially through the quality of our love and service. And we are to promote, foster, enable aliveness in all its dimensions. This is, I believe, an inspiring and vibrant way of understanding our mission.

TO GATHER INTO UNITY

A SECOND JOHANNINE MODEL emphasises the movement towards unity, the gathering into one. This topic is first broached in the discourse about shepherding, an image deeply rooted in biblical tradition (10:1-38). Jesus identifies himself as the Good Shepherd, who knows his sheep intimately and is concerned for them. In contrast to the hireling who, when danger looms, takes to flight to save his skin, Jesus is prepared to lay down his life for his sheep. He then continues:

> I have other sheep that do not belong to this fold. I must bring them also, and they will listen to my voice. So there will be one flock, one shepherd (10:16).

This vision of a single flock under one shepherd, found earlier in the prophets (see Micah 5:3-5; Jeremiah 3:15; 23:4-6; Ezekiel 34:23-24), implies that the love of Jesus unto death, and the abundant life which he has come to offer, are not restricted to the people of Israel. Others too will hear his voice. A new flock, a new community, comprising both Jew and Greek, will come into existence. This new unity reflects and is based on the oneness between Jesus and the Father (10:15,18,30).

Later, as John's plot unfolds, the Jewish religious leaders (*'the chief priests and Pharisees'*) in the wake of the enthusiastic response to the raising of Lazarus, call a meeting at which Caiaphas, the High Priest at the time, presides. This is the Johannine equivalent of the

Sanhedrin trial scene found in the Synoptic passion narratives, and omitted in the Johannine passion. [8] In fact, the whole of John's Gospel is considered by many scholars as the trial of Jesus. [9] The leaders are deeply disturbed by the large numbers rushing after Jesus; they are afraid that *'everybody will believe in him'*, and that this will result in the Romans taking decisive and destructive action against Temple and nation. At this point Caiaphas disparagingly highlights their lack of perception, and indicates that:

> "You do not understand that it is better for you to have one man die for the people than to have the whole nation destroyed." (11:50)

There is a touch of cynical pragmatism in Caiaphas' approach. Ironically, the phrasing suggests the thinking, current at the time, about the sacrifice of the Maccabaean martyrs, whose deaths saved Israel. The narrator continues:

> He did not say this on his own, but being high priest that year he prophesied that Jesus was about to die for the nation, and not for the nation only, but to gather into one the dispersed children of God (11:51-52).

The comment underlines that the effects of Jesus' death will be felt beyond the confines of Israel. Others right across the world, who are also children of God, will be drawn in, 'gathered' to form a new people, a new community.

Later in the narrative, after Jesus' entry into Jerusalem, the Pharisees note with some discouragement that *'the whole world has gone after him'* (12:19). This comment is followed by the arrival of some Greeks who have come to look for Jesus. Their request to see him, conveyed by Andrew and Philip, is taken as the sign that the 'hour' has now finally come, the hour of the glorification of the Son of man. There follows a scene which is the Johannine equivalent of the Synoptic agony in Gethsemane. There is the terror and anguish, the prayer to the Father, the surrender to the Father's will. Then Jesus exclaims:

> "Now is the judgment of this world; now the ruler of this
> world will be driven out. And I, when I am lifted up from
> the earth, will draw all people to myself." (12:31-32)

The 'gathering' of all to Jesus is the purpose and result of his being 'lifted up', his being raised on the cross, which is also his exaltation.

Finally, there is the prayer of Jesus at the supper:

> that they may all be one. As you, Father, are in me and I am
> in you, may they also be in us, so that the world may believe
> that you have sent me (17:21).

This vision of unity is found also in the opening hymn of the letter to the Ephesians, a hymn frequently recited in the Church's Office. In this hymn, which some scholars think may have originated in a baptismal liturgy, we praise and thank our God and Father for choosing us, for accepting us, for forgiving us, for freely lavishing his gifts upon us. We thank him also for letting us know the mystery of God's purpose, his overarching plan, namely:

> that he would bring everything together under Christ as
> head, everything in the heavens and everything on earth
> (1:10 NJB).

The picture is that of the restoration of God's rule to the whole universe as well as humankind. For the author of this letter it is clear that the clearest symbol of such unifying is the breaking down of the barrier between Jew and Gentile.

> But now in Christ Jesus you that used to be so far off have
> been brought close, by the blood of Christ. For he is the
> peace between us, and has made the two into one entity

and broken down the barrier which used to keep them apart by destroying in his own person the hostility, that is, the Law of commandments with its decrees. His purpose in this was, by restoring peace, to create a single New Man out of the two of them, and through the cross, to reconcile them both to God in one Body; in his own person he killed the hostility. He came to bring the good news of peace to you who were far off and peace to those who were near. Through him, then, we both in the one Spirit have free access to the Father (2:13-18 NJB).

The saving activity of Jesus is expressed in terms of a unifying which abolishes fundamental differences. In spatial terms the reconciliation obtained by Jesus' death is both horizontal and vertical. Through the gift of the Spirit all are drawn into equal relationship with God as Father, and incorporated into the one Christ, and thus brought into a new unity with one another across all divides. All are now the one people of God, the Church.

I have long felt drawn to this vision. I think that it was this passage which inspired Teilhard de Chardin, whom I admired in my student days. He envisaged the whole of creation as moving from chaos and utter disunity, moving upwards and inwards into greater unity. Christ is the rod or axis running through it all, drawing it together; and Christ is the climactic point to which this vast movement is directed.

At a personal level, a social or community level, a political level, a cosmic level, this model is extremely evocative. In this view of things, evil and sin can be seen in terms of existing disharmony, or the intro-duction of further disunity, or a falling back into dispersion and division, or a refusal to integrate, to grow into oneness, to advance to greater harmony. Mission, then, has to do with integrating and unify-ing, overcoming opposition and division, promoting what unites, fighting all that estranges and separates. For Teilhard, the energising force of this process is love.

What is also significant about this unity model of mission, is that such unity is the result of Jesus' death. This is evident in each of the passages which we have considered: the shepherd motif, the trial scene, the statement about being 'lifted up'. This indicates that unity is the gift of God, but is also costly for those involved. It suggests that our participation in this mission will entail considerable dying, like the wheat grain (12:24). For:

> Whoever serves me must follow me, and where I am, there
> will my servant be (12:26).

We shall later examine the implications of this for the celebration and living of eucharist.

TO PREACH AND EXORCISE

I WOULD LIKE TO TURN now to the Gospel of Mark. This Evangelist always presents the mission of Jesus beneath the twin rubric of proclaiming the Good News (his preaching and teaching), and casting out devils or exorcising. This is evident, for instance, in the opening day of his ministry in the Capernaum synagogue, where he preaches with authority, and then performs a spectacular exorcism (1:21-28). Shortly afterwards we find a typical Marcan summary which reads:

> And he went throughout Galilee, proclaiming the message
> in their synagogues and casting out demons (1:39).

Those called to discipleship share the same mission. For Mark, discipleship means to 'be with' Jesus and *'to be sent out to proclaim the message, with power to cast out demons'* (3:14-15).

We may feel a little uncomfortable with the concept of exorcising. I believe that by this term Mark intends the overcoming of evil in whatever form it occurs. This can be physical, psychological, or spiritual, as seen in the story of the paralytic (2:1-12). It can be personal, social, or institutional, as evidenced in episodes such as the healing of the leper (1:40-45), or the woman with the severe haemorrhage (5:25-34). Evil is present in natural phenomena like storms (4:35-41), and religious systems like the Temple (11:12-14, 20; 15:38). For Mark, evil is an indication that Satan still holds sway, and that the Kingdom has not yet come, that God is not yet reigning. Put in a more positive key, the mission of Jesus is to proclaim and to inaugurate the Reign of God. Through his words and deeds, the Reign of God comes near and can be experienced, bringing liberation, healing and transformation.

As disciples of Jesus we are sent to proclaim by our words (preaching, teaching, catechising, evangelising, counselling, affirming, encouraging, challenging...), and by the witness of our lives and our compassion God's nearness in saving love. We are to promote and foster the values of God's Kingdom, transforming life at every level and in every sphere. Mark had this vision of a great battle between Jesus and the power of evil. We in our day are in the thick of this battle too, as new dimensions of evil arise amidst the old. We are called to resist and confront this evil, to work for change, to offer alternatives, to create a different world.

TO BRING GOOD NEWS

IN LUKE'S GOSPEL, after the baptism and testing of Jesus, Jesus returns to Galilee, *'with the power of the Spirit in him'*.[10] Whatever he accomplishes in his ministry is done through the empowering Spirit. Before the summoning of any disciples he returns to his native Nazareth. It is known that he has switched from carpentry to preaching, and so he is invited to read in the synagogue on the Sabbath.

> 16 When he came to Nazareth, where he had been brought up, he went to the synagogue on the sabbath day, as was his custom. He stood up to read, 17 and the scroll of the prophet Isaiah was given to him. He unrolled the scroll and found the place where

it was written: *18*"The Spirit of the Lord is upon me, because he
has anointed me to bring good news to the poor. He has sent me
to proclaim release to the captives and recovery of sight to the
blind, to let the oppressed go free, *19*to proclaim the year of the
Lord's favour." *20* And he rolled up the scroll, gave it back to the
attendant, and sat down. The eyes of all in the synagogue were
fixed on him. *21* Then he began to say to them, "Today this scripture has been fulfilled in your hearing." (Luke 4:16-21)

It appears that Jesus chooses this passage from Isaiah. He makes this
prophetic dream, which encapsulates the yearnings of centuries, his
own dream, his way of articulating what he is about, his manifesto or
mission statement, as we would call it today. Jesus identifies himself
with the one spoken of by Isaiah; he is the anointed one; the Spirit
of the Lord is on him. As such he is sent to bring good news, proclaim liberty, to bring sight and freedom, to announce the Lord's year
of favour. The link between Spirit and mission is expressed very
closely here. (11)

Later, when approached by two of the Baptist's disciples, asking
whether he was the long expected one, he replies:

22 And he answered them, "Go and tell John what you have
seen and heard: the blind receive their sight, the lame walk,
the lepers are cleansed, the deaf hear, the dead are raised,
the poor have good news brought to them. *23* And blessed
is anyone who takes no offence at me." (7:22-23)

There is consistency between mission statement and realisation,
dream and reality. Jesus not only preaches Good News to the poor
and needy of all kinds, he is Good News. According to this model,
this is our mission too – to be individuals and communities whose
Spirit-filled presence is Good News, news which liberates, enlight-
ens, heals and makes people glad.

The Paraclete

AS WELL AS THE IMAGES of wind and water in connection with the Spirit, the Fourth Evangelist introduces another term, found in the New Testament only in the Johannine literature. It is the Paraclete, and it occurs in the material devoted to the Last Supper (ch.13-17). This term has several nuances. [12] Its basic meaning has a forensic ring: legal assistant, or advocate, or witness. This meaning is in keeping with the trial atmosphere which pervades John's narrative of the ministry of Jesus. The term also has links with the words used in early Christianity for preaching and exhortation (*paraklesis*). In the Septuagint, the Greek version of the Old Testament, it connotes consolation. In the discourse material of the Supper its meaning seems to be a combination of spokesperson, advocate, consoler, helper, counsellor, guide, protector. Given this complexity it is probably wiser to remain with the term Paraclete rather than choose one of these functions to the detriment of the others, as do some translations, including the one we are using in this volume. The Paraclete is identified with the Spirit, but the term has a more personal flavour.

The context of the final meal which Jesus has with 'his own' provides the occasion for his farewell discourse. The practice of placing a farewell speech or 'testament' on the lips of a great person or hero prior to his death is widespread in biblical literature. [13] It occurs, for example, in the case of Jacob (Genesis 47-50), Moses (Deuteronomy 31-34), David (1 Kings 2:1-10), Mattathias (1 Maccabees 2:49-70). There are also examples dating from two or three centuries after the death of Jesus. Such speeches include elements such as a prediction of coming death and departure, an exhortation to followers to conduct themselves in accordance with the style of the departing figure, predictions of future difficulties and dangers, a final commissioning which includes the command to love one another, the affirmation and renewal of God's Covenant, a final prayer of praise. Several of these elements are found in connection with the five passages of the Supper Discourse in which the term 'Paraclete' is used.

The heading which is commonly used for chapters 13-17, the Last Discourse, accurately reflects the narrative as we find it. But scholars detect several underlying discourses, perhaps originally homilies, which have been brought together: 14:1-31; 15:18-16:3; 16:4-33. This explains the repetition which is a characteristic feature of this material. The first two Paraclete passages are found in the first of these discourses.

Jesus, who is about to leave 'his own' and return to the Father seeks to reassure them. He is going away in order to prepare a place for them, so that they may be with him. He is the Way, Truth and Life, intimately at one with the Father to whom he is going. He then states:

> 15 "If you love me, you will keep my commandments.
> 16 And I will ask the Father, and he will give you another Advocate, to be with you forever. 17 This is the Spirit of truth, whom the world cannot receive, because it neither sees him nor knows him. You know him, because he abides with you, and he will be in you (14:15-17).

It is in a covenant context of love that Jesus promises to ask the Father to give the disciples 'another Paraclete', phrasing which suggests that Jesus himself is the first Paraclete (see also 1 John 2:1). This Paraclete will take over the role so far fulfilled by Jesus, and will stay with believers forever, unlike Jesus who is soon to depart. And so the Paraclete will be the ongoing presence of Jesus in his absence. The Paraclete is identified as the Spirit of Truth, the one who communicates the Truth, and will remain with them, dwell in them (see 6:56; 15:4-5 concerning the indwelling of Jesus). The Fourth Gospel presents Jesus as the unique revealer, the light of the world; Jesus has just claimed to be the Truth. The Paraclete will continue this revealing role, and in this way make present the ongoing mission of Jesus. But in the ministry Jesus as the light created a division, for some rejected the light and preferred darkness. Similarly, the Paraclete's presence will cause division. The Paraclete will not be recognised, known or accepted by the world, but will dwell in the disciples and keep alive in them the revelation of Jesus.

The second brief passage is more focused:

> 25 "I have said these things to you while I am still with you.
> 26 But the Advocate, the Holy Spirit, whom the Father will
> send in my name, will teach you everything, and remind
> you of all that I have said to you (14:25-26).

The Paraclete is here, and only here, explicitly identified with the Holy Spirit. Like Jesus the Paraclete is a 'Sent One', sent by the Father. Rather than at Jesus' request (14:16), the Paraclete is sent in Jesus' name, with the role of teaching the disciples everything, and reminding them of the things which Jesus has taught them already. So the Paraclete's role is not independent, nor does it entail the communicating of something new. Rather, it helps the disciples and believers to remember what Jesus has revealed, and come to understand it more clearly and penetrate it more deeply. In this way the mission of Jesus is continued. Earlier in the Gospel there have been occasions when Jesus has told his confused disciples that one day they would come to understand (2:22; 12:16); this will be the fruit of the Paraclete's presence after his departure.

The final words of chapter 14 give the impression that the Supper has come to a conclusion, for Jesus, after stating that he is acting in obedience to the Father and out of love for Him, says to his disciples: '*Come now, let us go.*' However, Jesus immediately continues to speak, embarking on a another discourse. This consists of two sections: the allegory of the vine and the branches, which includes the testament themes of love, mission and indwelling (15:1-17), and a passage which highlights the world's hatred (15:18-16:3).

> 26 "When the Advocate comes, whom I will send to you
> from the Father, the Spirit of truth who comes from the
> Father, he will testify on my behalf. 27 You also are to testi-
> fy because you have been with me from the beginning
> (15:26-27).

The immediate background here is one of hostility. Jesus reminds the disciples that the world has hated, persecuted and rejected him. He goes on to warn them that the world will hate and persecute them also, because they will be the bearers of his revelation to the world. They will be expelled from the synagogue, and even be put to death (16:2). Jesus therefore reassures them in the face of this crisis by promising to send them the Paraclete, again described as the Spirit of Truth. Like Jesus the Spirit is said to come from the Father, but in this passage will be sent by Jesus rather than by the Father at Jesus' request (14:16), for the Father and Jesus are one.

The aspect of the role which is now emphasised is that of witnessing, a theme of great importance in the Gospel of John. The Paraclete will bear witness to Jesus, but cannot be seen by the world, and so will witness through the witnessing of the disciples, who were with Jesus from the outset of the ministry (see Acts 1:21). Such witnessing will inevitably give rise to opposition, for the servants will share the Master's experience (15:20; 12:26). This motif of coming persecution and the consequent need to defend the Good News is found also in the Synoptic Gospels in what is usually referred to as the Eschatological Discourse, given by Jesus in the week prior to his passion (Mark 13; Matthew 24-25; Luke 21). There are also interesting parallels in an earlier discourse in Matthew in which Jesus is addressing his disciples before they embark on a local mission (see also Luke 12:12 in a different context).

> 17 Beware of them, for they will hand you over to councils and flog you in their synagogues; 18 and you will be dragged before governors and kings because of me, as a testimony to them and the Gentiles. 19 When they hand you over, do not worry about how you are to speak or what you are to say; for what you are to say will be given to you at that time; 20 for it is not you who speak, but the Spirit of your Father speaking through you (Matthew 10:17-20).

Opposition and persecution will normally accompany the Christian mission. But the Spirit/Paraclete, enlightening and sustaining the disciples, will bear witness through them to the good news and to the truth of Jesus.

The next section of the Last Discourse (16:4-33) is thought by many scholars to be an alternative or duplicate version of the discourse in chapter 14, for many of the themes are repeated. There are two references to the Paraclete, and although they run consecutively, the emphasis is different, and so it is best to treat them separately.

> 7 Nevertheless I tell you the truth: it is to your advantage that I go away, for if I do not go away, the Advocate will not come to you; but if I go, I will send him to you. 8 And when he comes, he will prove the world wrong about sin and righteousness and judgement: 9 about sin, because they do not believe in me; 10 about righteousness, because I am going to the Father and you will see me no longer; 11 about judgement, because the ruler of this world has been condemned (16:7-11).

Again the background is the departure of Jesus, his going to the one who sent him (16:5), a departure which is causing his disciples sadness of heart. Jesus explains to them that his departure will be good for them, and is essential if the Paraclete is to come. He assures them again that the vacuum created by his absence will be filled as a result of his sending the Paraclete to them. This time it is Jesus who, after his glorification, will himself send the Paraclete (7:39). Again the Paraclete is to be understood as the presence of the absent Jesus.

In these verses there is a new, forensic, emphasis to the role of the Paraclete, a role which extends beyond the Christian faith community. The Paraclete judges the world and demonstrates that the world is wrong. In the ministry the presence of Jesus as the light and the revelation of the truth inevitably served to expose the darkness and brought about judgement as people accepted or rejected him.

The Paraclete will act in a similar way. The verb used (*elenchein*) has a range of meanings: blame, convince, investigate, convict, expose, prove wrong. There are three moments of exposure or proving wrong. Firstly, the Paraclete will expose the world's sin, which consists in its refusal to believe in Jesus (3:19; 9:41; 12:37), a rejection which culminated in his being put to death. Secondly, the Paraclete will show that Jesus rather than his opponents is righteous. They have claimed to be the genuine children of Abraham, disciples of Moses, obedient followers of the Law, and accused Jesus of arrogance and blasphemy, executing him as guilty. In this they have failed to recognise Jesus as Son of the Father, the revelation of God. The Paraclete will make his vindication clear. Thirdly, the apparent victory of the prince of this world, the power of darkness and evil, acting through Jesus' enemies in his condemnation and execution, will be seen to be a false claim. In fact, the glorification of Jesus, his returning to the Father, proves that it is the prince of this world who stands condemned, and the judgement is reversed. In these three areas the Paraclete will enable the disciples to see the truth.

The other role of the Paraclete which is highlighted in this discourse recalls aspects already encountered.

> *12* "I still have many things to say to you, but you cannot bear them now. *13* When the Spirit of truth comes, he will guide you into all the truth; for he will not speak on his own, but will speak whatever he hears, and he will declare to you the things that are to come. *14* He will glorify me, because he will take what is mine and declare it to you. *15* All that the Father has is mine. For this reason I said that he will take what is mine and declare it to you (16:12-15).

As the Spirit of truth, the Paraclete will continue the revealing mission of Jesus. Since the disciples at the time are too fragile to cope with all that Jesus wants to communicate, the Paraclete will later guide and lead them into the fullness of truth (8:32). The disciples will be enabled to grasp and understand the wider implications and depths of the revelation which Jesus has brought, and thus will be empowered to continue his mission. Just as Jesus was not the source of what he revealed, but was dependent on the Father, so the Paraclete will not speak of his own accord, but will recall what Jesus has said. *'Things to come'* does not, then, refer to new revelation (15:15). The Paraclete will point the disciples forward, indicating what will flow from the 'hour' of Jesus, his death and exaltation, until the end of time, and interpreting for coming generations the contemporary significance of what Jesus has said and done. In this way will the Paraclete also glorify Jesus, make known his mystery and identity, his oneness with the Father (1:1-2). All that Jesus has he has received from the Father; this the Paraclete will declare to the disciples.

Across these five passages the main emphasis presents the Paraclete, who is the Spirit of Truth, in a guiding, enlightening, teaching, reminding role. The secondary meaning, which has closer contact with the Synoptic tradition, is couched in judging and forensic terms, and probably developed in the light of the Johannine community's experience of conflict, rejection and suffering.

Pentecost

IN DISCUSSING THE GIFT OF THE SPIRIT there is a key text which we need to address. It contains Luke's version of the initial outpouring of the Spirit on the new Christian community.

> *1* When the day of Pentecost had come, they were all together in one place. *2* And suddenly from heaven there came a sound like the rush of a violent wind, and it filled the entire house where they were sitting. *3* Divided tongues, as of fire, appeared among them, and a tongue rested on each of them. *4* All of them were filled with the Holy Spirit and began to speak in other languages, as the Spirit gave them ability (Acts 2:1-4).

It seems that on the next pilgrimage feast after the Passover on which

Jesus died, his Galilean disciples came to Jerusalem for the celebration, and during this time the presence of the Spirit, as promised by Jesus prior to his ascension (Luke 24:49), was manifested. This occasion of their baptism by the Holy Spirit was taken as the sign that as the official witnesses of Jesus they should begin the public proclamation of all that God had done through him. (14)

Originally, the Jewish Pentecost was a thanksgiving feast for the harvest. In time it had come to be linked with the Exodus, and had become the commemoration of God's giving the Law to Moses on Sinai, and the establishment of the covenant with Israel. This was the moment when Israel was called to be God's own people. Perhaps Luke received the tradition which connected this feast with the first public proclamation of the Good News, and he dramatised it using echoes of the imagery of the Exodus account (Exodus 19:16-19; 20:18), such as the noise like wind and the tongues like fire as perceptible signs of the presence of the empowering Spirit (Psalms 104:4; 28:7LXX). Philo, a Jewish writer contemporary with Luke, comments that at Sinai God's voice divided into seventy tongues, and every nation heard the Law in their own language. For Luke, the Jews who witness the immediate effect of the Pentecost event in Jerusalem have returned to the city from all over the Roman Empire. This symbolises the international outreach which will follow, and anticipates the inclusion of Gentiles in this new people.

Just as the Spirit anoints Jesus for mission at the baptism, so the Spirit becomes the source of the life and mission of the newly covenanted people of God. The Spirit will guide and enliven this people in its development and outreach.

After this event the book of Acts provides us with Peter's inaugural sermon. The response to this we considered at the beginning of the last chapter - repentance and baptism, to the tune of three thousand people. Luke goes on to describe aspects of how these people lived (Acts 2:42-47). This is the first of several 'summaries' (4:32-37; 5:12-16), which paint rather idealised pictures of the foundational community.

42 They devoted themselves to the apostles' teaching and

fellowship, to the breaking of bread and the prayers. [43] Awe came upon everyone, because many wonders and signs were being done by the apostles. [44] All who believed were together and had all things in common; [45] they would sell their possessions and goods and distribute the proceeds to all, as any had need. [46] Day by day, as they spent much time together in the temple, they broke bread at home and ate their food with glad and generous hearts, [47] praising God and having the goodwill of all the people. And day by day the Lord added to their number those who were being saved (Acts 2:42-47).

Four key elements can be identified in this passage. Firstly, there is the term *koinonia*, sometimes translated as 'fellowship', but really meaning 'communion', or 'common union', a communal manner of life. It is the first term used to designate the Christian community, and expresses the deep bonds existing between the baptised because they share the common Spirit. The Spirit creates and sustains a oneness in the Risen Jesus which is at the same time a profound oneness with each other. This term captures our identity as Church. One feature of 'communion' in that initial Christian grouping was the sharing of material possessions, which is a striking sign of commitment. Perhaps Luke generalises what may have been exceptional acts of generosity. (15)

Secondly, the early Christians were a praying community. They probably continued initially to use their familiar Jewish prayers, like the psalms and the Shema. But they composed their own prayers and hymns as well. A number can be detected in Paul's letters (e.g. Philippians 2:6-11; Colossians 1:15-20), and some scholars believe that the *Magnificat, Benedictus and Nunc Dimittis* were early christian compositions which Luke took over and adapted for the Infancy narrative. (16) The same may be true of the Prologue in John. The early Christians also continued to frequent the Temple for worship.

The third feature is their gathering for the breaking of bread, and this we shall consider in a later chapter. Fourthly, they sought to live according to the teaching of the apostles. This item links with the commission in Matthew and the issue of characteristic ethos which was a topic for our reflection in the previous chapter.

Conclusion

IN CONCLUSION I would like to emphasise three elements from the reflections of this chapter.

TO BE ALIVE

THE IMAGES OF WATER AND WIND/breath highlight the Spirit's role as source and giver of life, and Jesus speaks of his coming that we might have life in all its fullness (John 10:10). John V. Taylor writes: "It has long been my conviction that God is not hugely concerned as to whether we are religious or not. What matters to God, and matters supremely, is whether we are alive or not." [17]   The Spirit quietly works to bring us more fully alive, making us more aware of the beauty of the natural world in which we live, more sensitive to the richness, originality and mystery of the human beings whom we encounter, more in touch with what is going on within us, more open to the splendour and tragedy of human experience, and more interested in its many facets and shades, more alert to human need at all levels of society, and prompts us to respond. The Spirit awakens us to God's presence in and through all this.

Vatican 2 reminded us that we are all called to holiness, a call which perhaps fails to set the adrenalin flowing. Rephrased as the call to aliveness in all its dimensions, it can, I believe, grasp our attention and stimulate our enthusiasm. Sadly, as individuals and Church, we can resist the Spirit's prompting, for to be so aware and responsive, to become fully alive, can be extremely painful and demanding. Taylor suggests that most of us opt to be a little blind, a little deaf, a little dead. We prefer to be quietly comfortable and safe. We resist the

Spirit; we fail to reach our potential as God's children. The celebration of the sacrament of confirmation offers an opportunity for all involved to renew their baptismal choice of life and to explore its exciting implications rather than to settle for the banal comfort of partly living.

MISSION AND WITNESS

The Spirit anoints and empowers us for mission. The context of the sacrament of confirmation, as we celebrate it in today's Church, provides an opportunity to reconsider the mission element of our Christian calling. Mission is not an additional extra, an appendix; it is central to our very being as followers of Jesus. The scriptural paradigms which we have considered offer rich insight into the mission of Jesus, and provide a range of ways in which we can understand what we are about. We will perhaps find some more attractive, meaningful and challenging than others. It is, I believe, very useful to attempt to spell out in a few telling phrases our own 'mission statement', the key elements of our responding to what God's love is demanding of us in our world. In this it is important not to forget that Christian mission has to do with being as well as doing.

Another concept linked with mission is 'witness'. The Spirit empowers us to witness to the person and values of Jesus. Such witnessing can be costly. As Christians we are in a minority today. The values which dictate policy at all levels of society are frequently at variance with the values of the Gospel. The atmosphere of secularism and the pressures of consumerism are pervasive. It is difficult to live our Christian truth in integrity. It is distinctly uncomfortable to be made to feel different, a little 'odd' and irrelevant, to be marginalised even. The Spirit/Paraclete is the source of wisdom and courage as we seek to face this challenge.

The characteristic prayer given to us by Jesus addresses God as

'Abba', Father, and this leads inevitably to pray that the Kingdom may come more fully into our own lives and communities, and the wider world. In making that prayer we commit ourselves to work for the fulfilment of this dream; we pledge ourselves to mission and to witness.

GROWTH IN KNOWLEDGE AND UNDERSTANDING

THE THEME OF WATER as symbol of both Spirit and revelation, and several of the Paraclete sayings, highlight our need to deepen our understanding of the mystery of Jesus, his identity and role. The Spirit/Paraclete is the reminder, the teacher, the guide. For our part, we have a responsibility to read and reflect upon the scriptures, to pray and to study, so that under the Spirit's guidance we may not only come to know the mystery of God revealed in Jesus, but also be better equipped to communicate the Good News to others. This is an ongoing process, and is at the heart of our coming more fully alive.

These elements of aliveness, mission, witness, and growth in knowledge, which are linked to the Spirit's presence and action in our lives, are clearly aspects of the sacrament of baptism, as it is presented in scripture. From a pastoral viewpoint, confirmation allows us to highlight them at what is generally a later stage in our faith journey. Both sacraments are received only once, but they introduce us into an ongoing and developing way of being and living which embraces every aspect of our existence.

NOTES

(1) In Acts 8:14-18 we see that the gift of the Spirit is linked with the laying on of hands by the apostles; this takes place after an earlier baptism but is linked with it. In 19:5-6 a number of Ephesians are baptised by Paul in the name of the Lord Jesus; Paul lays hands on them and the Holy Spirit then comes down on them and they begin to speak with tongues and to prophesy.

(2) Helpful commentaries on Genesis include: R. Davidson, *Genesis* (Cambridge, CUP 1973); M. Maher MSC, *Genesis* (Wilmington, Glazier 1982); E.A. Speiser, *Genesis* (New York, Doubleday 1981); G. von Rad, *Genesis – a Commentary* (London, SCM 1972); G.J. Wenham, *Genesis 1-15* (Waco Texas, Word Books 1987).

(3) On Ezekiel I have found the following useful: A. Cody OSB, *Ezekiel* (Wilmington, Glazier 1984); M. Greenberg, *Ezekiel 21-37* (New York, Doubleday 1997); W. Eichrodt, *Ezekiel* (London, SCM 1970).

(4) See W. Eichrodt, *Ezekiel*, p. 502.

(5) In addition to the commentaries mentioned in chapter 1, note 8, see L.P. Jones, *The Symbol of Water in the Gospel of John* (Sheffield, SAP 1997).

(6) For the background of the Jewish feasts at the time of Jesus see: G.A. Yee, *Jewish Feasts and the Gospel of John* (Wilmington, Glazier 1989).

(7) See I. De la Potterie, *The Hour of Jesus* (Slough, St. Paul 1989), p.152-156. On the passion narratives see R.E. Brown, *The Death of the Messiah* (London, Chapmans 1994), 2 vols; *A Crucified Christ in Holy Week* (Collegeville, Liturgical Press 1986); also D. Senior, *The Passion of Jesus in the Gospel of John* (Leominster, Gracewing 1991).

(8) Elements of the content of the Synoptic trial scene are found in different contexts in John. In 2:19 we find the saying concerning the destruction and replacement of the Temple (Mk.14:58); in 10:24-25 the 'Jews' ask Jesus to tell them openly if he is the Messiah (the question posed by the High Priest in Mk.14:61). In 10:33-36 the Jews intend to stone Jesus for blasphemy because of his claim to be the Son of God; in Mark (14:64) Jesus is condemned for blasphemy for the same affirmation, to which he has added a promise to come again as Son of Man, a promise found in Jn.1:51.

(9) See, for example, A.E. Harvey, *Jesus on Trial. A Study in the Fourth Gospel* (London, SPCK 1976).

(10) On Luke see: G.C. Caird, *St. Luke* (London, Pelican 1963); E.E. Ellis, *The Gospel of Luke* (London, Oliphants 1974); C.F. Evans, *Saint Luke* (London, SCM 1990); J.A. Fitzmyer, *The Gospel according to Luke* (New York, Doubleday, vol 1 1981, vol 2 1985); L.T. Johnson, *The Gospel of Luke* (Collegeville, Liturgical Press 1991); I.H. Marshall, *The Gospel of Luke* (Exeter, Paternoster Press 1978); D. McBride, *The Gospel of Luke* (Dublin, Dominican Publications 1991).

(11) See also the baptism (3:22), the introduction to the temptation scene, where the Spirit is twice mentioned (4:1), and the summary before Jesus' visit to Nazareth (4:14).

(12) See R.E. Brown, *John*, vol 2, p.1135-43.

(13) See F.J. Moloney, *John*, p.376-378.

(14) See R.E. Brown, A *Once-and-Coming Spirit at Pentecost*, p.9; also the books referred to in chap 1 note 1. The view that the disciples left Jerusalem after the death of Jesus and returned to Galilee and there encountered the Risen Lord, and subsequently came back to Jerusalem does not follow the Lucan version of events (Lk.24:36-53).

(15) See L.T. Johnson, *Acts*, p. 59.

(16) As well as the commentaries on Luke cited above, note 10, see R.E. Brown, *The Birth of the Messiah* (London, Chapmans 1978); A *Coming Christ in Advent* (Collegeville, Liturgical Press 1988), p.49-54.

(17) John V. Taylor, *A Matter of Life and Death* (London, SCM 1986), p.18.

CHAPTER THREE

Reconciliation

THE THEME OF FORGIVENESS and reconciliation
is central to the Good News, as we saw in
chapter one. The mission of Jesus has to do with
communicating God's forgiveness, and making
that forgiveness available in an ongoing manner
through the Church. For us today, this gift of
forgiveness is bestowed in the first place in the
sacrament of baptism. It is continued and
renewed through the sacraments of reconciliation
and eucharist. In this chapter we shall examine
scriptural texts which proclaim the gift of
forgiveness more widely understood than the
liturgical sacrament of reconciliation, though
they are relevant to that sacrament too. We shall
also discover hints of the beginnings of
sacramental practice in the early Church.
Our reflection will include the Kingdom of God
announced and made present by Jesus, table
fellowship in Luke, a Marcan narrative, the
mission to hand on reconciliation, and our call
to be a forgiving community.

The Wider Context of the Kingdom

WHEN LOOKING AT THE SCRIPTURAL BACKGROUND to reconciliation it is important to be aware of the wider context. After his baptism and subsequent testing in the wilderness, Jesus goes to Galilee and embarks on his ministry. Mark puts it this way:

> *14* Now after John was arrested, Jesus came to Galilee, proclaiming the good news of God, *15* and saying, "The time is fulfilled, and the kingdom of God has come near; repent, and believe in the good news." (Mark 1:14-15)

The central theme of Jesus' preaching was undoubtedly the message that God was beginning to establish his sovereignty over his creation, his people and the whole world. Jesus believed that the long awaited time had come, and that Israel's God was breaking into history in a decisive way through his ministry; he was God's prophet, called to lead this movement of renewal and salvation.

The concept of Kingdom is extremely rich and multifaceted. [1]   It is drawn from the story of Israel: God's choice of a people, their Exodus liberation from the oppression of Egypt, their desert journey and the key event of Sinai, their entry into the Land of Promise, the later resplendent kingship of David, the establishment of Jerusalem and the building of the Temple as Yahweh's dwelling place. It is also a story of failure: there were many bad kings, prophets from Yahweh were ignored, the people was frequently unfaithful in many ways, the city and Temple were destroyed, and the people taken into exile. Subsequently, there arose a dream for the future: Yahweh would intervene in their history again; there would be a merciful restoration that would include the return from exile, a rebuilt Jerusalem with a new purified Temple, a renewed people, the subjection of the Gentiles, and the conquest of evil. Jesus draws on this story, its imagery and language, and fashions something new and original and challenging from that heritage.

Jesus articulated his dream about the kingdom or reign of God in parables and prayers, in prophetic statements and beatitudes. He made this dream a reality, something to be experienced, through his exorcisms and healings, and through symbolic gestures like the lakeside banquet and the cleansing of the Temple. His call for repentance was, in the first place, a summons to national reconversion, a becoming once again the true Israel, and was linked with the people's theological return from exile. It is within this broader context that individual conversion must be situated.

With the call to conversion came the offer of forgiveness. The Old Testament prophets linked the return from exile and renewal of the covenant with the forgiveness of Israel's sins, which had occasioned the exile in the first place (see Jeremiah 31:31-34; 33:4-11; Ezekiel 36:24-26,33; Isaiah 52-55). Jesus was proclaiming that the time for Israel to be forgiven was finally present. His word of forgiveness to individuals, spoken in his own name and outside the existing system, which was linked with the Temple, is part of the bigger picture. They are thereby included in the restored people of God, they are embraced by the dawning reign of God.

One of the characteristic features of Jesus' ministry, a gesture which both proclaimed and made real the Kingdom, was his habit of sharing his table with all kinds of people, and extending a welcome to 'sinners'. Of the Evangelists Luke explores the theme of Jesus' table fellowship to the greatest effect.

Table Fellowship in Luke

IN THE COURSE OF HIS GOSPEL Luke presents Jesus taking meals with sinners and people on the fringes of society. Jesus dines also with the religious elite, whatever their motives for inviting him. Meals provide the topic for some of his parables, and the setting for important teaching. The context for both post-resurrection encounters is a meal. I have selected four meal narratives for our consideration. (2)

THE CALL OF LEVI

THE FIRST OCCASION which Luke records follows the call of Levi early in Jesus' ministry:

> ²⁹ Then Levi gave a great banquet for him in his house; and there was a large crowd of tax collectors and others sitting at the table with them. ³⁰ The Pharisees and their scribes were complaining to his disciples, saying, "Why do you eat and drink with tax collectors and sinners?" ³¹ Jesus answered, "Those who are well have no need of a physician, but those who are sick; ³² I have come to call not the righteous but sinners to repentance." (Luke 5:29-32)

Jesus sees Levi seated at his tax office and invites him to follow him, and thus break decisively with his normal way of life. His job probably entailed collecting the customs dues on goods arriving into the kingdom of Herod Antipas. Besides affording lucrative opportunities for extortion, it necessitated frequent contact with Gentile merchants and officials. So his whole profession was stigmatised, and its participants were regarded as the dregs of Jewish society.

In order to mark the occasion of his entering into the 'following' of Jesus, Levi holds a big reception for him in his house, inviting his colleagues and friends and many others with whom no respectable Jew would wish to associate. They share table fellowship with Jesus and he with them. The Pharisees and their scribes take umbrage at this disregard for the accepted standards and, presumably some time later, question Jesus' disciples about their eating and drinking with such appalling company. Jesus springs quickly to their defence and explains why it is that he welcomes 'sinners'. He uses a medical proverb: people who are in good health do not require a doctor; it is the sick who experience such a need. A doctor's responsibility demands his presence with those who are suffering, not self-quarantined avoidance of possible contagion. Jesus asserts, not without a touch of irony, that his mission is concerned primarily not with those who consider themselves righteous, but with 'sinners', folk who are aware of their need for healing and forgiveness.

SEEKING AND FINDING

LATER IN LUKE'S GOSPEL there is a similar incident.

> *1* Now all the tax collectors and sinners were coming near to listen to him. *2* And the Pharisees and the scribes were grumbling and saying, "This fellow welcomes sinners and eats with them." (15:1-2)

The marginalised and religious outcasts in large numbers are drawing close to Jesus; their purpose is to listen to him, which for Luke is an indication of an openness to conversion (5:1,15; 6:17,27,47,49; 7:29; 8:8-18; 9:35; 10:16,24,39; 11:28,31). In the background are the religious elite, the 'Pharisees and scribes', who keep their distance to avoid contamination, and shun table fellowship with sinners. They 'grumble' repeatedly and openly. Their criticism is focused not only on Jesus' eating and drinking with these people, as on earlier occasions (5:30; see 7:34), but also on his welcoming them, his offering hospitality. To host or entertain sinners was a more serious offence to the scribes and Pharisees than simply to eat with sinners informally or to accept invitations, which was itself scandalous enough.

In that culture to share table was a very significant gesture. It was a sign of acceptance, respect and trust, an offer of peace, fellowship and friendship. To share table indicated a being 'at home' with others, a willingness to share life, an identification and oneness with them; it was an expression of solidarity. Jesus' action bridged the social and religious divide in a culture extremely conscious of status and class and prestige. It showed the sinners and outcasts that they mattered to him, that they had a value. It was a healing and liberating event. Since Jesus was looked upon as in some way a man of God, a prophet, his gesture of friendship communicated and experienced through table fellowship, would have been understood as an indication of God's acceptance and forgiveness. Through the welcome he extended, "he was declaring on his own authority that anyone who trusted in him and his kingdom-announcement was within the kingdom." [3] This gesture is the most powerful parable of the kingdom; it proclaims the message and makes present the reality of God's nearness in saving love.

The great scripture scholar Jeremias writes that "the inclusion of sinners in the community of salvation, achieved in table fellowship, is the most meaningful expression of the message of the redeeming love of God." [4] I believe that we can affirm that this symbolic gesture contains the whole Gospel, the Good News, in a nutshell. [5]

In Luke's narrative the response of Jesus to the criticism of the Pharisees is to explain his attitude and conduct by recounting three parables. There are two short parables presented in parallel and carefully matched: the parables of the lost sheep and the lost coin. Then there is the longer and very familiar parable of the two lost sons, normally and misleadingly referred to as the parable of the prodigal son. In fact, I think that the usual emphasis on lostness in these parables is misplaced. In the Lucan context I prefer to see them as parables of seeking and finding that which is lost, a seeking which is demanding and costly, and a finding which calls for joyful celebration.

The twinned parables, which reflect Luke's typical interest in equal opportunities, with male and female protagonists, build on our human experience of losing things which are important to us, and taking great efforts to find them, and the joy and satisfaction which discovering them brings. Jesus is saying that God is no less persistent in seeking nor less jubilant in finding. God sets a high value on the lost, and spares no effort to recover it. One aspect which I find fascinating is that Jesus chooses as pointers to the depths of God's being a shepherd and a woman. To tend sheep was a low-class occupation, a role avoided by religious people; it was one of the proscribed trades; one carrying it out would be considered a 'sinner' by the religious elite! Women in that cultural milieu suffered religious and social discrimination, and had very little value. Yet, a member of each of these groups is put forward by Jesus as an image of God. Another significant point is the fact that the sheep and the coin do not do anything; the seeking and the finding are gift. For Jesus the emphasis is not on conversion, but on God's gratuitous searching love.

So Jesus bases his ministry on his understanding of the mind and heart of God. He takes his cue from that knowledge. His table fellowship is his way of articulating his mission. It is revelation of God and of God's purpose.

The classic longer parable which brings the trilogy to a climax is probably the best known and loved of all Jesus' parables. Both sons are lost, one in a far, foreign pig-sty, the other at home on the farm. The parable tells of the prodigal, extravagant love of the father as he searches for them both. The younger he finds, and there is a celebration. The older? We are left to wonder.

The key word in the whole parable, or key phrase in translation, is, I believe, the verb which describes the father's response when he catches sight of the returning younger son in the distance:

> So he set off and went to his father. But while he was still
> far off, his father saw him and was filled with compassion;
> he ran and put his arms around him and kissed him (15:20).

All that follows in the narrative springs from compassion. The father runs to meet his son. Normally an elder would not run; it was socially unacceptable. But it enables him to meet the young man outside the village boundary and protect him from the inevitable hostility of the villagers. A remarkable reconciliation takes place. The father says nothing; there is no lecture or blame or criticism. But his actions express his profound love, acceptance and welcome. He kisses him repeatedly in a firm embrace, a sign of forgiveness, a recognising that he is his son, and this is public, for all the villagers to see. The son forgets the crippling hunger which prompted his decision to return, and abandons his plan of maintaining his independence as a hired servant. He comes to realise that what is at issue is a broken relationship, a relationship which he cannot heal. The possibility of that relationship being re-established can only come as a pure gift from his father. The young man perceives from his father's behaviour that such an offer is being made. The father's compassionate love brings about a change within him, and he graciously accepts the gift freely and generously offered, beyond his wildest dreams.

When the other son returns from the fields and gets wind of the party, he reacts angrily and refuses to join the meal prepared. He remains outside, which is a public insult to his father. The father's response is to come out of the house and to plead with him. He comes in search of his older son. The latter's response reveals the extent of his alienation. There is no respect, no affection; he complains bitterly, betraying the attitude of a slave rather than a son. He is self-righteous about his impeccable obedience, disparagingly critical of his father's other son whom he refuses to acknowledge as his brother. Obviously, he is quite incapable of understanding and entering into his father's joy. From the father there is no outburst of anger, no criticism, no recall to duty. Rather, he reaches out, searching to bridge the gulf between them – *'My son, all I have is yours'*.

The parable responds magnificently to the initial context. The sinners are sharing the banquet, found by the searching Jesus. The religious leaders stand critically aloof, refusing the invitation to accept the Good News and join the party. The table fellowship of Jesus is a celebration of seeking and finding. The three parables reflect the way in which Jesus understands his ministry, what he is about. At the same time these parables reveal a great deal about Jesus' understanding of God. Jesus operates in the way he does, shares table fellowship as he does, because he knows the compassionate heart of his Father, his "all-inclusive, unconditional love, his unreserved acceptance and approval". [6] Table fellowship expresses it all.

THE WOMAN IN SIMON'S HOUSE

RESPECTING LUKE'S EQUAL OPPORTUNITY POLICY I have chosen two other Lucan episodes which take place in the context of a meal. The first is the story of the sinful woman in the house of Simon, a member of the religious elite. The story is preceded by the comment that Jesus had a reputation for being a friend of tax gatherers and sinners (7:34).

> 36 One of the Pharisees asked Jesus to eat with him, and he went into the Pharisee's house and took his place at the table. 37 And a woman in the city, who was a sinner, having learned that he was eating in the Pharisee's house, brought an alabaster jar of ointment. 38 She stood behind him at his feet, weeping, and began to bathe his feet with her tears and to dry them with her hair. Then she continued kissing his feet and anointing them with the ointment. 39 Now when the Pharisee who had invited him saw it, he said to himself, "If this man were a prophet, he would have known who and what kind of woman this is who is touching him— that she is a sinner." 40 Jesus spoke up and said to him, "Simon, I have something to say to you." "Teacher," he replied, "Speak." 41 "A certain creditor had two debtors; one owed five hundred denarii, and the other fifty.
> 42 When they could not pay, he cancelled the debts for both of them. Now which of them will love him more?" 43 Simon answered, "I suppose the one for whom he cancelled the greater debt." And Jesus said to him, "You have judged rightly." 44 Then turning toward the woman, he said to Simon, "Do you see this woman? I entered your house; you gave me no water for my feet, but she has bathed my feet with her tears and dried them with her hair. 45 You gave me no kiss, but from the time I came in she has not stopped kissing my feet. 46 You did not anoint my head with oil, but she has anointed my feet with ointment. 47 Therefore, I tell you, her sins, which were many, have been forgiven; hence

she has shown great love. But the one to whom little is forgiven, loves little." [48] Then he said to her, "Your sins are
forgiven." [49] But those who were at the table with him
began to say among themselves, "Who is this who even for-
gives sins?" [50] And he said to the woman, "Your faith has
saved you; go in peace." (7:36-50)

This Pharisee named Simon invites Jesus to dine with him. He obviously respects Jesus as a rabbi, a prophet even, and perhaps finds
aspects of his teaching attractive. His welcome is polite, but, as we
learn later, lacks the gestures which are special signs of warmth and
hospitality. Having left his sandals at the door, Jesus is reclining on a
divan. Usually the door was left open, and sometimes beggars would
come in to pick up the scraps, or admirers to relish the conversation.
On this occasion, the person who enters is a woman who was living
an immoral life in the town, who had come to hear that Jesus was at
table in the Pharisee's house. Maybe there had been some direct
contact between them previously, or perhaps "she had seen and
heard him from the fringe of the crowd, and that had been enough to
soften the hardness of her heart and to set her back on the road to
self-respect". [7] Alternatively, she may have been led to repentance
and the beginning of a new life through some indirect knowledge of
Jesus and his message. We are not told. Her intention was probably
to use the perfume to anoint his head as a sign of gratitude, but her
emotions get the better of her and she breaks down in floods of tears
which wet Jesus' feet. Without thinking, she lets down her hair,
which is quite unacceptable in public, to wipe his feet dry; she
kisses and anoints his feet. One can imagine Simon's embarrassment!

"Through all this," writes Caird, "Jesus did not turn; for he had no
need; all that he needed to know about the uninvited guest he could
read in the mirror of Simon's shocked face, and all he needed to do
for the woman he could do by accepting motionless the homage of
her penitent love." [8] What Jesus in fact read was:

> If this man were a real prophet, he would know who this woman
> is who is touching him, and what a bad character she is (7:39).

The words imply that he did not know, and that, had he been aware, he would have withdrawn from contact with her.

In fact Jesus shows that he does know; she is a sinner, but a repentant and pardoned sinner. Then, through a parable about little and large debts freely cancelled, he brings out the significance of her actions and the contrasting dispositions of his host. He gently points out to Simon, not his lack of basic courtesy or failure to do what was necessary, but his economical love. There was no foot bath, no kiss of friendship, no oil of respect. These the woman has substituted abundantly, effusively, with great love and unrestrained, spontaneous affection and gratitude, which reveal the pardon she has come to acknowledge.

There is some discussion amongst scholars as to whether the sense of the text is that the woman's manifestation of love towards Jesus brings her forgiveness, or that her love is a consequence of her having been already forgiven, though this has not been recorded. The latter position, in which the parable is integrated into the narrative, is the view which I have followed.

This is a moving narrative of two-way love. The woman shows so many signs of a love which is far from 'economical', and Jesus accepts her with great respect, allowing her to express her feelings, and even touch him. He welcomes the service she renders, and allows her to remain close to him, refusing to send her away even though the cultural and religious expectations warrant it and even though the atmosphere is pulsating with shock and disapproval. Her love and faith are in such contrast with the cold, self righteous, closed and withdrawn attitude of the male, religious elite.

ZACCHAEUS

THE SECOND STORY concerns one of the 'little people' of the New Testament, Zacchaeus.

1 He entered Jericho and was passing through it. *2* A man was there named Zacchaeus; he was a chief tax collector and was rich. *3* He was trying to see who Jesus was, but on account of the crowd he could not, because he was short in stature. *4* So he ran ahead and climbed a sycamore tree to see him, because he was going to pass that way. *5* When Jesus came to the place, he looked up and said to him, "Zacchaeus, hurry and come down; for I must stay at your house today." *6* So he hurried down and was happy to welcome him. *7* All who saw it began to grumble and said, "He has gone to be the guest of one who is a sinner."
8 Zacchaeus stood there and said to the Lord, "Look, half of my possessions, Lord, I will give to the poor; and if I have defrauded anyone of anything, I will pay back four times as much." *9* Then Jesus said to him, "Today salvation has come to this house, because he too is a son of Abraham. *10* For the Son of Man came to seek out and to save the lost." (19:1-10)

Zacchaeus is described as the *'superintendent of taxes'*, an unusual term which probably indicates a responsibility for the collecting of customs dues on goods passing into Judaea from Peraea, and from further East. He has evidently benefited from the financial possibilities which such a post in a city like Jericho offered, for he is said to be extremely wealthy. However, *'he was eager to see what Jesus looked like'*, having heard no doubt of Jesus' reputation in his treatment of people like him. His desire must have been more than mere Herodian curiosity (9:9). Caird speculates that it may have included a desire to escape from his self-imposed loneliness, the social ostracism which went with the job, to break free from a profession now burdening his conscience. (9) So he climbs up a sycamore tree to get a view, since his smallness of stature precludes that possibility amidst the crowd.

The spotlight now focuses on Jesus. It is he who, in response to Zacchaeus' interest, seizes the initiative. Jesus is aware of his presence, looks up at him, calls him by name, and invites himself to a meal and lodging in his home:

> "Zacchaeus, be quick and come down, for I must
> stay at your house today." (19:5)

There is a note of urgency in his words. Zacchaeus is delighted. This is more than he has ever envisaged. So he climbs down with alacrity and welcomes Jesus gladly. He is obviously touched by the graciousness of Jesus and his spontaneous offer of fellowship, and all that this implies.

By contrast, the bystanders are scandalised by the fact that Jesus has chosen to be the guest of 'a sinner', and they voice their disapproval. For to their way of thinking, to share his table and home is to share his sin. Jesus frequently breaks through the barriers of religious prejudice with great freedom, and such freedom is a problem for others. As far as Zacchaeus is concerned, this freedom "awakened to vibrant life impulses that had long lain dormant and revealed to him the man he was capable of becoming." [10]   In response to Jesus' graciousness, and also to exonerate him from the crowd's suspicion, Zacchaeus declares that he turns his back decisively and without delay on his past:

> "Here and now, sir, I give half my possessions to charity;
> and if I have defrauded anyone, I will repay him four times
> over." (19:8)

Without any prompting from Jesus, Zacchaeus implicitly acknowledges his guilt, professing his intention to offer alms beyond the normally expected twenty per cent, and to pay restitution far in excess of the legal prescription. This is a clear illustration of conversion, that change of heart and ways which is the genuine response to Jesus. Jesus is quick to recognise and affirm this in his concluding words, which are addressed to both Zacchaeus and the crowd:

> "Today salvation has come to this house – for this man too
> is a son of Abraham. The Son of Man has come to seek and
> save what is lost." (19:10)

Zacchaeus is a genuine son of Abraham like any other Jew. The gift of salvation has been extended to him also. This final comment of Jesus sums up the scene, as it sums up his whole ministry. The language is that of the parables referred to earlier; it is the language and imagery of the Shepherd. Table fellowship is an initiative of saving and forgiving search, a reaching out to the 'outcast'; it is an expression of the nature of his mission.

A Marcan Incident

ONE OF MY FAVOURITE GOSPEL STORIES connected with reconciliation is found in Mark. It takes place in a house, but not at table.

> *1* When he returned to Capernaum after some days, it was reported that he was at home. *2* So many gathered around that there was no longer room for them, not even in front of the door; and he was speaking the word to them. *3* Then some people came, bringing to him a paralysed man, carried by four of them. *4* And when they could not bring him to Jesus because of the crowd, they removed the roof above him; and after having dug through it, they let down the mat on which the paralytic lay. *5* When Jesus saw their faith, he said to the paralytic, "Son, your sins are forgiven."
> *6* Now some of the scribes were sitting there, questioning in their hearts, *7* "Why does this fellow speak in this way? It is blasphemy! Who can forgive sins but God alone?"
> *8* At once Jesus perceived in his spirit that they were discussing these questions among themselves; and he said to them, "Why do you raise such questions in your hearts? *9* Which is easier, to say to the paralytic, 'Your sins are forgiven,' or to say, 'Stand up and take your mat and walk'? *10* But so that you may know that the Son of Man has authority on earth to forgive sins" – he said to the paralytic – *11* "I say to you, stand up, take your mat and go to your

home." ¹² And he stood up, and immediately took the mat
and went out before all of them; so that they were all
amazed and glorified God, saying, "We have never seen
anything like this!" (Mark 2:1-12)

In the story of the paralytic we find a controversy about forgiveness
enclosed within the framework of a healing miracle. This results in a
dramatic and compelling presentation of the nature of the Kingdom.
It is whilst Jesus is characteristically proclaiming his message to the
pressing crowds that the paralytic is lowered into his presence.
Moved by the tenacious ingenuity, determination and faith of his
friends, and doubtless also by their affection for the poor sufferer,
Jesus, with authority and warmth, speaks the word of forgiveness:
'My son, your sins are forgiven', the prophetic announcement of the
in-break of the Kingdom, God's reign in love, into the contorted
frame of the paralytic's life, assuring him of the gift of God's unconditional, saving acceptance.

This forgiving word is uttered within the context of an act of healing.
The man is paralysed, a helpless cripple. His physical affliction
entails further disabilities: he cannot live a normal family life; he cannot work and earn a living; nor can he take part in the political,
social and religious life of the community to which he belongs. It is
also a pointer to a more radical need and disability, his need for God,
his sin, his poverty of being. In that culture, physical misfortune was
often considered to be the result of sin. It is this poverty that Jesus
comes to enrich and transform. When approached for a cure, it is to
this more fundamental and urgent need that, with intuitive empathy,
he turns his attention first. *'My son, your sins are forgiven'*.

The effect and effectiveness of his prophetic word of forgiveness are
illustrated by the ensuing physical cure.

> "I order you: get up, pick up your stretcher, and go off
> home." And the man got up, and at once picked up his
> stretcher, and walked out in front of everyone.

The man is restored to bodily wholeness. He can stand erect, bend and carry; he can hike, and work in the fields, and saw wood; he can stand to his waist in the water and cast a net And his feelings, his feelings of guilt, inadequacy, frustration, anger, failure, and resentment, feelings which must have weighed heavily or torn him apart, are dissipated like the early morning mist. He is restored to his family and the life of the local community. A new day has dawned. All this reflects that deeper wholeness, new life and fellowship which is the full reality of the Kingdom. For, as Morna Hooker comments, "forgiveness and healing are not here two distinct acts, but are different aspects of one thing – the total restoration of the paralysed man. The one guarantees the other... because they belong together." [11]

This episode must serve as one example of the many acts of healing which Jesus performed, summarised in his response to the disciples of the Baptist.

> 2 When John heard in prison what the Messiah was doing, he sent word by his disciples 3 and said to him, "Are you the one who is to come, or are we to wait for another?" 4 Jesus answered them, "Go and tell John what you hear and see: 5 the blind receive their sight, the lame walk, the lepers are cleansed, the deaf hear, the dead are raised, and the poor have good news brought to them. 6 And blessed is anyone who takes no offence at me." (Matthew 11:2-6)

Jesus' reply echoes the dream about God's coming to save his people expressed in Isaiah 35:5-6. His healing activity is not only an expression of compassion and deep humanity. These individuals were not only broken and damaged, their sickness and deformities excluded them from full membership of Israel. His healings are signs of a new inclusiveness, pointers to the reality of the Kingdom coming to birth, the restoration and renewal of the community of Israel. Healing and forgiveness are part of the blessings accompanying the advent of the Kingdom. [12]

Handing on this Reconciliation

THE GOSPEL TEXTS which we have considered illustrate the way in which Jesus during his ministry forgave sins within the wider context of national reconciliation. After his death the early Christians, as we saw in chapter one, proclaimed God's offer of forgiveness extended to both Jews and Gentiles. This means that in telling the story of Jesus the Evangelists' major concern is not to relate his words and deeds simply as past facts. They intend to proclaim the perennially gladdening news and enduring meaning of the event of Jesus, his ongoing offer of healing, fellowship and forgiveness.

THE COMMISSION IN RESURRECTION APPEARANCE NARRATIVES

THERE ARE TWO resurrection appearance narratives in which the Risen Lord explicitly gives his followers the mandate to communicate the message and gift of forgiveness. As we saw earlier, one of the basic elements in a resurrection narrative is a commissioning. Those who encountered the Risen Jesus came away from the experience with a firm conviction of 'being sent'. The way this conviction is articulated and formulated within the narrative owes a great deal to the individual evangelist's theological perspective.

In the Lucan version, the Risen Jesus appears to the assembled apostles and their companions in Jerusalem on Easter Day after the Emmaus couple have rejoined them. After wishing them *'Peace'*, he endeavours to dispel their agitation and doubts by proving that he is not a ghost. He invites them to see his hands and feet, thus establishing a link with the crucifixion, and he eats some grilled fish. Then he seeks to enlighten them about the meaning of the scriptures in his regard, especially the message of suffering and resurrection, about which he spoke to them in the ministry. He concludes:

> 46 ..."Thus it is written, that the Messiah is to suffer and to rise from the dead on the third day, 47 and that repentance and forgiveness of sins is to be proclaimed in his name to all nations, beginning from Jerusalem. 48 You are witnesses of these things. 49 And see, I am sending upon you what my Father promised; so stay here in the city until you have been clothed with power from on high." (24:46-49)

It is precisely after the Pentecostal outpouring of the Spirit promised here that Peter tells the hearers of his inaugural sermon that they need to repent and be baptised for the forgiveness of sins. The forgiveness which Jesus showed in his ministry now on his authority becomes the heart of the mission of the Church as recounted in Acts (2:38; 3:19; 5:31; 13:38). It is offered not only to the Jews, but also to the Gentiles, *'to all nations'*, in accordance with his command (Acts 10:43; 13:46; 26:16-18). This mission is understood to be the fulfilment of God's overarching plan expressed in the Old Testament. The gift of forgiveness is communicated through preaching and baptism.

In the Gospel of John we find a similar treatment. We looked in the last chapter at the resurrection appearance in John 20, concentrating on the way Jesus sends the disciples forth on mission as he has been sent by the Father, and for this he breathes on them and gives them the Spirit. His accompanying words are:

> "Receive the Holy Spirit. If you forgive the sins of any, they are forgiven them; if you retain the sins of any, they are retained." (20:22-23)

During his ministry as the Fourth Evangelist presents it, the presence of Jesus inevitably creates a crisis; people are obliged to make the decision to come to the light and the life or to turn away and remain in death and darkness. In the discourse at the Supper, as we have seen, Jesus describes the mission of the Paraclete in similar terms; one facet is to lay bare the goodness and evil of the world (John 16:7-11). The disciples through the gift of the Spirit now have the mission to make the absent and exalted Jesus present in the world with his ongoing offer of light and life, and so inevitably their proclamation provokes this fundamental decision of acceptance or rejection, and the judgement whereby sins are forgiven or retained. A positive response of acceptance opens the believer to that initial gift of forgiveness linked with baptism, as in Luke. Some scholars believe that a continuing exercise of forgiveness within the community may also be implied by Jesus' words.

THE COMMUNITY OF 1 JOHN

IT IS GENERALLY ACCEPTED that the Fourth Gospel was finalised some sixty or so years after the resurrection of Jesus. (13) In that time the community had grown and developed, and problems had also arisen. The document commonly referred to as the First Letter of John, written a few years later at the turn of the century, probably by a different author than that of the Gospel but a member of the same 'school', seeks to address some of these issues. The following passage is pertinent to our theme:

> 5 This is the message we have heard from him and proclaim to you, that God is light and in him there is no darkness at all. 6 If we say that we have fellowship with him while we are walking in darkness, we lie and do not do what is true; 7 but if we walk in the light as he himself is in the light, we have fellowship with one another, and the blood of Jesus his Son cleanses us from all sin. 8 If we say that we have no sin, we deceive ourselves, and the truth is not in us. 9 If we confess our sins, he who is faithful and just will forgive us our sins and cleanse us from all unrighteousness. 10 If we say that we have not sinned, we make him a liar, and his word is not in us.

> 1 My little children, I am writing these things to you so that you may not sin. But if anyone does sin, we have an advo-cate with the Father, Jesus Christ the righteous; 2 and he is

the atoning sacrifice for our sins, and not for ours only but
also for the sins of the whole world (1 John 1:5-2:2).

It appears that a group of believers had seceded from the Johannine
community. Claiming to base themselves on the Gospel of John, they
evinced a different moral outlook and espoused a different christol-
ogy from that of the tradition. The author of 1 John is anxious to limit
the effects of their propaganda on the other members of his community. In this carefully balanced passage he presents a version of their
views in three conditional sentences, each of which is followed by a
conditional sentence in which he rejects their tenets, presenting the
official interpretation and view of the community.

Basically, the secessionists maintain that after baptism it is faith that
matters; their moral behaviour is of no consequence for salvation.
Therefore they do not consider wrongdoing as sinful. The author
considers their position symptomatic of the realm of darkness and
deception and untruth. In rejoinder he advocates that the members
of the community recognise the presence of sin in their lives. Ideally
after baptism there should be no place for sin, and naturally he
wishes to prevent their sinning. But he is conscious of undeniable
unfaithfulness in the community. However, he proclaims that the
cleansing power of forgiveness which comes through the atoning
death of Jesus is permanently effective and available. The Lamb of
God continues to take away our sins (see John 1:29). As our advocate (or Paraclete) at the Father's side, Jesus continues to plead for us,
and God remains faithful and merciful.

The context for the receiving of this forgiveness is the community (John
20:23). Sin offends God, but it has a negative effect on the 'communion' of the group. Following a tradition found in the Old Testament
(Proverbs 28:13; Sirach 4:25-26; Leviticus 5:5-6; Daniel 9:20), when
the author speaks of 'acknowledging' or 'confessing' sins in verse 9, he
probably means a public avowal in the presence of the community,
possibly in a liturgical context.

The question of post-baptismal sin is raised again later in the document:

> 16 If you see your brother or sister committing what is not a mortal sin, you will ask, and God will give life to such a one – to those whose sin is not mortal. There is sin that is mortal; I do not say that you should pray about that. 17 All wrongdoing is sin, but there is sin that is not mortal (1 John 5:15-17).

There has been much scholarly discussion about the sin described here as 'mortal' or 'deadly'. It probably refers to those who have left the community, and created a schism, the secessionists. They have adopted a basic orientation of non-belief in Jesus as the Christ come in the flesh, and do not recognise the saving effect of his death; they show no real love for the other members of the community. In becoming Christians they passed from death to life (1 John 3:14); they have now opted for darkness and death and belong to the 'world' (humankind opposed to Christ). Their situation is not unlike those who are guilty of 'an eternal sin' because they have blasphemed against the Holy Spirit in blinding themselves to God's presence in Jesus (Mark 3:29). In addition to discouraging prayer for the secessionists, the author later advocates that there should be no contact with them, in order to prevent their further contaminating the community (2 John 10-11).

The main thrust of the passage, however, is positive and exudes hope and confidence. Members of the community who are alive with God's life, 'eternal life' (1 John 5:13), are assured that their prayer for sinful members will be favourably heard by God; forgiveness and life will be given to the sinner. The letter of James too links prayer with forgiveness; it also recommends confession of sins to one another in the community (James 5:13-16).

PAUL

PAUL HAD TO DEAL with similar issues some fifty years earlier and nowhere more urgently than in the community which he founded at Corinth. His second letter to that community contains the following passage:

17 So if anyone is in Christ, there is a new creation: everything old has passed away; see, everything has become new! *18* All this is from God, who reconciled us to himself through Christ, and has given us the ministry of reconciliation; *19* that is, in Christ God was reconciling the world to himself, not counting their trespasses against them, and entrusting the message of reconciliation to us. *20* So we are ambassadors for Christ, since God is making his appeal through us; we entreat you on behalf of Christ, be reconciled to God (2 Corinthians 5:17-20).

This is a most beautiful extract, profoundly theological. The language of reconciliation is found in the New Testament only in Paul's writings. (14) The term provides a way alternative to justification, redemption or salvation to describe what God has done through the death and resurrection of Jesus, and at the same time it suggests yet another way of articulating Christian mission. Verses 18 and 19 are carefully balanced. Scholars think that 19 is taken from traditional material. In the first part of each verse the emphasis is on the initiative of God; the offer of reconciliation is God's action, God's gift. And this takes place in and through Jesus Christ.

The second part of each verse focuses on the mission, the ongoing responsibility of the reconciled to proclaim what God has done and what God is offering, and so to be agents or ministers of reconciliation. Paul clearly claims that this describes his own apostolic mission, but it is applicable to other evangelists and all believers. This ministry Paul goes on to describe as being *'ambassadors of Christ'*. An ambassador comes with the authority of the one sending him. The hearers, for their part, are invited to respond, to be open to the gift offered, to allow themselves to be reconciled.

The initial effect of reconciliation, when Paul first converted the Corinthians some years previously (50-51 AD), is described in verse 17. There was a radical transformation; they have become new creatures, they exist 'in Christ' – concepts which we discussed in the chapter on baptism. In the meantime some of the members of the community have experienced difficulty in living according to the values inculcated by Paul, and their behaviour has caused concern. A rift has also developed between Paul and some of the community. So in the current letter he is appealing for them to 'be reconciled' to God and to himself, to be reconverted, to embrace again the Gospel which he preached to them some years before, lest their previous acceptance of God's grace come to nothing (6:1).

Earlier in the letter Paul refers specifically to the painful situation which had arisen in his last visit to the community. It seems that an individual insulted him in public in a way which undermined his authority, and the other members of the community failed to rally to his defence. In a letter written after leaving them, but which is no longer extant, Paul appears to have insisted that the person responsible be punished. The community responded positively, reprimanding him and imposing a penalty, probably some form of exclusion from the life of the community and from the eucharist (see also 1 Corinthians 5:1-5 for a similar situation). Now Paul writes:

> 6 This punishment by the majority is enough for such a person; 7 so now instead you should forgive and console him, so that he may not be overwhelmed by excessive sorrow. 8 So I urge you to reaffirm your love for him. 9 I wrote for this reason: to test you and to know whether you are obedient in everything. 10 Anyone whom you forgive, I also forgive. What I have forgiven, if I have forgiven anything, has been for your sake in the presence of Christ. 11 And we do this so that we may not be outwitted by Satan; for we are not ignorant of his designs (2 Corinthians 2:6-11).

Paul's current preoccupation is that the man, who has recognised his fault and repented, be forgiven and welcomed back into the community with warmth. It is interesting that the members of the community, as well as Paul, have had a role in the process of discipline and reconciliation. Their forgiveness and his coincide. Here and in 1 John we have a glimpse of the early Church beginning to develop ways of handling the ongoing forgiveness of sinful members.

A Forgiving Community

ONE OF THE MAIN CHARACTERISTICS of the new community, the renewed and restored Israel, which Jesus was establishing, was that it should be a forgiving and healing community. The link between being forgiven by God and extending forgiveness to others is repeatedly made by Jesus. One of the kingdom parables recorded by Matthew affords a classic example:

> 23 "For this reason the kingdom of heaven may be compared to a king who wished to settle accounts with his slaves. 24 When he began the reckoning, one who owed him ten thousand talents was brought to him; 25 and, as he could not pay, his lord ordered him to be sold, together with his wife and children and all his possessions, and payment to be made. 26 So the slave fell on his knees before him, saying, 'Have patience with me, and I will pay you everything.' 27 And out of pity for him, the lord of that slave released him and forgave him the debt. 28 But that same slave, as he went out, came upon one of his fellow slaves who owed him a hundred denarii; and seizing him by the throat, he said, 'Pay what you owe.' 29 Then his fellow slave fell down and pleaded with him, 'Have patience with me, and I will pay you.' 30 But he refused; then he went and threw him into prison until he would pay the debt.
>
> 31 When his fellow slaves saw what had happened, they were greatly distressed, and they went and reported to their lord all that had taken place. 32 Then his lord summoned him and said to him, 'You wicked slave! I forgave you all that debt because you pleaded with me. 33 Should you not have had mercy on your fellow slave, as I had mercy on you?' 34 And in anger his lord handed him over to be tortured until he would pay his entire debt. 35 So my heavenly Father will also do to every one of you, if you do not forgive your brother or sister from your heart." (Matthew 18:23-35)

Matthew devotes the fourth of the five blocks of discourse material in his Gospel to issues concerning discipline and relationships within the Christian community (18:1-19:1). He includes Jesus' warning against leading the weaker members of the community astray and despising the 'little ones'. He locates here the parable of the Lost Sheep, suggesting that the leaders of the community must seek out those who have strayed. There follows a section (v.15-20) which has close links with some of the issues discussed above. It suggests a process of correction for community members who have sinned, and entertains the eventual possibility of exclusion from the community based on the power of 'binding and loosing' invested in the community. (15)   The parable follows.

The topic of forgiveness is introduced by Peter who asks Jesus how often he is to forgive his brother if he goes on wronging him. He himself suggests as many as seven times, doubtless thinking himself quite magnanimous in extending the number from the rabbinic four times to seven. The reply of Jesus must have stunned him: *"Not seven, I tell you, but seventy times seven"*. In other words, there is to be no limit at all to our forgiving.

In the parable by which Jesus illustrates his teaching the high-ranking minister owes the king an enormous amount which runs into millions. There is no way that he can possibly pay back the debt. In response to his plea the master *'was so moved with compassion that he released him and forgave him the debt'*. The verb used is the technical verb, found also in the Lucan parables of the father seeking his two sons and the good Samaritan; it denotes deep compassion, a compassion which moves to action. The king's compassion leads to extraordinarily generous forgiveness which is bestowed as a free gift. The forgiven servant then comes across a fellow-servant who owes him a paltry amount, and treats him with unyielding harshness. The lesson is clear and challenges all of us: *"I forgave you all that debt because you pleaded with me. Should you not have had mercy on your fellow slave, as I had mercy on you?"* The proclamation of the Kingdom is the offer of the free gift of God's compassionate forgiveness; those embraced by the Kingdom, those who have received this gift and been drawn into the new family of Jesus, are called to demonstrate the same compassionate forgiveness to others, *'from your heart'*.

The parable expresses in story form the fifth petition of the Lord's prayer, which is found in Matthew's Gospel at the centre of the sermon on the mount. *"Forgive us the wrong we have done, as we have forgiven those who have wronged us"* (6:12 NEB). Human forgiveness and divine are correlatives; refusal to forgive others is an obstacle to the reception of the forgiveness of the Father. Matthew adds a further saying to the prayer:

> *14* For if you forgive others their trespasses, your heavenly Father will also forgive you; *15* but if you do not forgive others, neither will your Father forgive your trespasses (6:14-15).

At an earlier point in that sermon, which Wright understands as the proclamation of a radically new way of being the true Israel, [16] Matthew includes another telling statement of Jesus:

> *23* So when you are offering your gift at the altar, if you remember that your brother or sister has something against you, *24* leave your gift there before the altar and go; first be reconciled to your brother or sister, and then come and offer your gift (5:23-24).

Presumably, Jesus had temple worship in mind when he uttered these words; Matthew would apply them to his own community – and to us. Worship cannot be divorced from daily life. Mark records a similar saying:

> "Whenever you stand praying, forgive, if you have anything against anyone; so that your Father in heaven may also forgive you your trespasses." (Mark 11:25)

Openness to forgive is part of the definition of the new family of God. *'Be generous to one another, sympathetic, forgiving each other as readily as God forgave you in Christ* (Ephesians 4:32).

Conclusion

THE THEME OF RECONCILIATION as presented in scripture is compellingly moving and disconcertingly challenging. I suggest three concluding considerations.

FORGIVEN AND FORGIVING

THE GIFT OF FORGIVENESS offered by Jesus takes us to the heart of his mission, the establishing of the Reign of God. It reveals the compassionate heart of God, who searches for us, reaches out to us in love, renewing and transforming our humanity. We are reminded of our basic human poverty and sinfulness, our constant need for healing and forgiveness. We are invited to trust in God's faithfulness and enduring love, to believe that God will not let us go (John 10:29; Romans 8:38-39). Perhaps we need also to recapture the sense of wonder which can be dulled by routine and familiarity, as time and time again Jesus through the word of the Church breaks into the shell of our lives and with gentle authority and assurance speaks to us the message of reconciliation and hope: 'My child, your sins are forgiven'. As forgiven and reconciled people, forgiveness is to be the hallmark of the Christian community, a clear sign of the presence of the Kingdom. The forgiveness freely given in baptism and frequently celebrated in the sacrament of reconciliation impels us to live as forgiving and healing people. Conflict surrounds us at all levels of society, and reminds us how urgent, demanding and elusive reconciliation can be. It is not absent from our own Church communities. Our mission is to be ambassadors of reconciliation, inviting others too to open themselves to God's gift, and promoting healing and peace, understanding and reconciliation at all levels of human interaction.

HEALING

IN THE MINISTRY OF JESUS forgiveness and healing went together in the establishing of the Kingdom. As Christians, inadequate and still in need of healing, we are called to be ministers of healing for others. Aspects of this ministry are specialised, and there is need within the Christian community for trained counsellors and spiritual directors. But other aspects of this ministry are simply facets of Christian aliveness. We can all listen, extend hospitality and a space 'to be'; we can all affirm, support and encourage, be compassionate, offer genuine warmth and friendship. Such humanity can help dispel hurt and bitterness, alleviate depression and loneliness, restore confidence, hope and the ability to trust, help people become more whole and more fully alive. As individuals and as Church communities we are intended to know the embrace of God's healing and forgiveness and enable others to experience it in their own lives.

TABLE FELLOWSHIP

When discussing the theme of meals in Luke, I suggested that the symbolic gesture of table fellowship contains the whole Gospel in a nutshell. Through sharing table with those considered sinners and outcasts Jesus revealed his understanding of God and of the nature of his mission. We cannot, therefore, avoid asking who the 'sinners' and outcasts are in our society today, the despised, the written-off, the fringe members, the voiceless minorities. As disciples on mission we are obliged to find ways of reaching out to them, ways of seeking and finding them, and enabling them to see the face of the God of Jesus, and to experience God's closeness and love touching their lives. As individuals and as Church, we need to show vision, creativity and courage in fashioning ways of making present in our contemporary world the realities of which Jesus' table fellowship was a sign: unreserved acceptance, genuine respect, hospitality, forgiveness, friendship. Scripture poses disconcerting questions, and offers an uncomfortable critique of our attitudes and responses and of some of our structures.

NOTES

(1) I am particularly indebted to J.P. Meier, *A Marginal Jew*, vol 2, p.241. His thorough and detailed treatment of the Kingdom theme runs from p.237-506; and N.T. Wright, *Challenge*, p.18-33; *Jesus and the Victory of God*, p.198-474.

(2) On Luke see the books recommended in chap 2 note 10; also, on this theme, M.T. Winstanley, *Into Your Hands* (Homebush, St. Paul 1994), p.89-110; *Come and See* (London, DLT 1985).

(3) N.T. Wright, *Jesus*, p.274.

(4) J. Jeremias, *New Testament Theology* (London, SCM 1971), p. 116.

(5) My understanding of Luke 15 has been greatly enriched by K.E. Bailey, *Poet & Peasant, and Through Peasant Eyes* (Grand Rapids, Eerdmans 1984), p.142-206. See also J.R. Donahue, *The Gospel in Parable* (Philadelphia, Fortress 1988), p.146-161.

(6) P. Tournier, *Guilt and Grace* (London, Hodder and Stoughton 1962), p.189.

(7) G.B. Caird, *Luke*, p.114.

(8) G.B. Caird, *Luke*, p.114.

(9) G.B. Caird, *Luke*, p.208.

(10) G.B. Caird, *Luke*, p.208.

(11) M.D. Hooker, *The Son of Man in Mark* (London, SPCK 1967), p. 89.

(12) See N.T. Wright, *Challenge*, p.47.

(13) On the Letters of John see: R.E. Brown, *The Epistles of John* (London, Chapmans 1983); P. Perkins, *The Johannine Epistles* (Dublin, Veritas 1979).

(14) The noun here in v.18&19; Romans 5:11: 11:15; and the verb here in 18, 19 & 20; Romans 5:10; 1 Corinthians 7:11; a compound verb is found also in 1 Corinthians 7:1; Ephesians 2:16; Colossians 1:20, 22. A list of useful books on 2 Corinthians is found in chap 1, note 15. 'Handing on reconciliation' is an alternative model for Christian mission (see the previous chapter on confirmation).

(15) The process envisages private correction as a first step, then correction in the presence of witnesses. If this fails the whole community comes together. If their appeal is rejected, the individual is excommunicated. The decision will be endorsed by God. J.P. Meier, *Matthew*, p.205, suggests that the procedure is based on the Old Testament (Leviticus 19:17-18; Deuteronomy 19:15), and reflects the Jewish origin of Matthew's community.

(16) N.T. Wright, *Jesus*, p.287-92.

CHAPTER FOUR

Eucharist

ONE OF THE FEATURES of the nascent Christian
community according to Acts, as we saw in
chapter two, was their gathering for the
breaking of bread (Acts 2:42). Our final chapter
is devoted to this theme, the sacrament of the
eucharist. The topic flows easily from that of the
previous chapter, reconciliation, because
reconciliation is an important aspect of the
scriptural presentation of eucharist. Both are
closely connected also by the key symbolic
gesture of table fellowship. We shall reflect
firstly on Gospel passages: Mark's narratives of
the multiplication of the loaves and fishes and
the Last Supper, the Johannine Supper narrative
and Bread of Life discourse, and two
resurrection narratives. Then we shall examine
some Pauline material. Finally, we shall draw
some conclusions about the implications of all
this for our Christian living, our sacramental
spirituality.

The Gospel of Mark

I WOULD LIKE TO BEGIN with Mark's Gospel. [1] There are two episodes in Jesus' ministry which are clearly linked, the multiplication of the loaves and fishes and the Last Supper, both of them influenced by the eucharistic experience of the Marcan church. The multiplication story is found in all four Gospels, a rare occurrence for Gospel narratives. In Mark and Matthew there are, in fact, two accounts of Jesus' multiplying activity, one in which the recipients number five thousand, the other in which the clientele is slightly smaller, numbering four thousand. In general, scholars maintain that the second story is probably an alternative version or 'doublet' of the first, rather than a separate incident in the ministry of Jesus.

THE MULTIPLICATION OF THE LOAVES AND FISHES

AS MARK TELLS HIS STORY, the two multiplication narratives, whatever their origin, need to be considered *in tandem* and also within the context of his wider plot. Jesus has called a group '*to be with him*', to share his life and values and vision, and '*to be sent*', to share his mission of proclaiming the Good News and overcoming the power of evil (3:13-19). They have accompanied him, listening to his message and receiving special instruction (4:1-34) and witnessing his 'mighty works' (4:35-5:43). They have not, however, always understood the meaning of his words or the significance of his actions. After the debacle of Nazareth (6:1-6) Jesus sends them forth on a limited mission to preach and exorcise, bearing his authority (6:7-13). When they return from their missionary expedition, they gather round Jesus and report with great excitement what *they* have said and done. The phrasing suggests that they overlook the fact that the source of their effectiveness is Jesus, not their own abilities.

Jesus, perceiving that they need a break, invites them to a quiet and isolated spot for a rest. The people, however, seem to guess their plan and thwart the attempt by reaching their intended destination before them. When Jesus sees the crowd, he is moved to compassion, *'because they were like sheep without a shepherd'*, in need of his saving message (Numbers 27:17; Ezekiel 34:5-6). So he spends a considerable time teaching and instructing them. The narrative continues:

> 35 When it grew late, his disciples came to him and said, "This is a deserted place, and the hour is now very late; 36 send them away so that they may go into the surrounding country and villages and buy something for themselves to eat." 37 But he answered them, "You give them something to eat." They said to him, "Are we to go and buy two hundred denarii worth of bread, and give it to them to eat?" 38 And he said to them, "How many loaves have you? Go and see." When they had found out, they said, "Five, and two fish." 39 Then he ordered them to get all the people to sit down in groups on the green grass. 40 So they sat down in groups of hundreds and of fifties. 41 Taking the five loaves and the two fish, he looked up to heaven, and blessed and broke the loaves, and gave them to his disciples to set before the people; and he divided the two fish among them all. 42 And all ate and were filled; 43 and they took up twelve baskets full of broken pieces and of the fish. 44 Those who had eaten the loaves numbered five thousand men (Mark 6:35-44).

The story is told in a way intended to forge links with Israel's past. The wilderness setting, the crowd's hunger, the more than adequate food supply, and the satisfied participants, recall the Exodus desert incident when Yahweh provided manna for the people, the bread from heaven (Exodus 16:1-35; Numbers 11:7-9). The companies of fifties and hundreds recall the marching groups on that desert journey. The Exodus, the liberation of Israel from slavery, was God's foundational saving event, and led to the establishment of Israel as God's own covenanted people. With the passing of the years, it came to be understood also as a pointer to the future. One strand of rabbinic messianic expectation included the hope of a Messiah like Moses who would again give the people manna to eat (see Psalm 132:15). The shepherd theme, introduced as Jesus steps ashore, is continued in the reference to the green grass where a table is prepared. Jesus is like Moses in his teaching and in his feeding. Both are aspects of the shepherding role, and raise the deeper question of Jesus' identity.

Another background strand is the dreaming of the prophets as they looked forward to a new age of God's saving closeness, and often used the image of a banquet at which the Messiah would preside (Isaiah 55:1f; 65:13f). The time of God's decisive intervention would be characterised by plentiful supplies of food and wine (Joel 3:18; Amos 9:13).

> 6 On this mountain the Lord of hosts will make for all peoples a feast of rich food, a feast of well-aged wines, of rich food filled with marrow, of well-aged wines strained clear. 7 And he will destroy on this mountain the shroud that is cast over all peoples, the sheet that is spread over all nations; 8 he will swallow up death forever. Then the Lord God will wipe away the tears from all faces, and the disgrace of his people he will take away from all the earth, for the Lord has spoken (Isaiah 25:6-8).

So the original incident behind Mark's narrative may have been intended by Jesus as a symbolic gesture, a sign that these dreams were being fulfilled, the messianic era was dawning, the Kingdom was present. It is worth noting that the banquet imagery and idea of messianic abundance are features of the story in John's Gospel when at Cana in Galilee Jesus provides wine instead of water. The enormous supply of superior quality wine is a sign that the new age has arrived in Jesus (John 2:1-11).

Mark's narrative also carries strong echoes of the episode in the book of Kings when the great prophet Elisha fed a hundred men with twenty barley loaves.

> *42* A man came from Baal-shalishah, bringing food from the
> first fruits to the man of God: twenty loaves of barley and
> fresh ears of grain in his sack. Elisha said, "Give it to the
> people and let them eat." *43* But his servant said, "How can
> I set this before a hundred people?" So he repeated, "Give
> it to the people and let them eat, for thus says the Lord,
> 'They shall eat and have some left.' " *44* He set it before
> them, they ate, and had some left, according to the word of
> the Lord (2 Kings 4:42-44).

The two available items of food, the prophet's command, the servant's hesitant question, the prophet's insistence, and the leftovers are all points of contact between the two narratives. In John's version of the multiplication (6:1-15) there is explicit reference to 'barley loaves', and it is a boy, not the disciples, who provides the loaves and fishes. The term which John uses to describe him is the same as that used for Elisha's servant.

The action in Mark's narrative is initiated by the disciples, who tell Jesus that it is getting late and suggest that he send the people away so that they can find provisions. But Jesus instructs them to provide the required food themselves. They respond with scant respect and on a practical level, pointing out the financial implications of this idea, and failing to grasp the point of Jesus' suggestion. Having ascertained that the disciples have some bread and fish with them, Jesus arranges the crowds as for a banquet. He then performs the central action: he takes the five loaves and two fish, raises his eyes to heaven, pronounces a blessing, breaks the loaves, and then involves the reluctant disciples in the distribution. Whilst it is true that the actions are those of the head of a family or a host at a meal, the narrative looks forward to Mark's later description of the Last Supper (14:22). Both consciously reflect the eucharistic experience of the reader. The distribution of the fish seems almost an afterthought. The collecting of twelve baskets of leftovers after feeding five thousand illustrates the magnitude of the miracle, but it also suggests a further eucharistic nuance. The existence of 'leftovers' (*klasmata*) indicates that the bread is still available into the future, whereas the manna in the desert had to be consumed from day to day (Exodus 16:19-20). The number twelve recalls the twelve tribes of Israel and the composition of the inner group of disciples who have been involved in the incident. The word 'men', used to describe the crowd, reflects the Jewish patriarchal society. The term used for baskets (*kophinoi*) is considered by some scholars to denote a specifically Jewish type of basket.

Jesus then compels the disciples to take to their boat and head for the other side of the lake, whilst he sends the crowds away and goes off to the hills to pray. He later comes to them across the water as they struggle against the wind and heavy sea. They cry out in fear, but Jesus calms their fears and calms the wind. *'Courage. It is I. Do not be afraid.'* Many scholars understand the narrative as a kind of epiphany in which Jesus uses the classic phrase from the Old Testament through which Yahweh revealed himself to the people: *'I am'* (Exodus 3:14; Isaiah 41:4). In exercising dominion over the forces of wind and sea Jesus performs an action which in the Jewish mentality was characteristic of God. [2] This fact, and his solemn self-identification, draw out the implications of the multiplication narrative. The disciples, however, remain dumbfounded. The narrator adds: *'They had not seen what the miracle of the loaves meant; their minds were closed'* (6:52). There are scholars who maintain that this episode is not historical, but was created by the early Church as a narrative commentary intended to bring out the theological and eucharistic implications of the multiplication story. In the eucharistic liturgy the risen and exalted Jesus comes to his followers in their fear, darkness and struggles, offering them comfort and reassurance. Such an interpretation would have been particularly apposite for a community suffering persecution and coming to terms with the impending or completed destruction of Jerusalem. [3]

Mark's second version of the multiplication occurs in a different setting. There is a controversy with Pharisees from Jerusalem which arises from the conduct of the disciples, who eat without washing their hands. Jesus gives greater emphasis to inner cleanness, and manifests a more liberal approach to purity laws. He then moves away into Gentile territory, where he is approached by a Syro-Phoenician woman who falls at his feet with a plea that he drive out a devil from her daughter. The dialogue which precedes his eventual acceding to her request continues the eucharistic theme and is paradigmatic for the whole thrust of this section of the Gospel (6:6-8:26).

> He said to her, "Let the children be fed first, for it is not fair to take the children's food and throw it to the dogs." But she answered him, "Sir, even the dogs under the table eat the children's crumbs." (7:27-28)

For Mark the point at issue seems to be the acceptance of Gentiles at the eucharistic table. The words of Jesus acknowledge the priority of the Jews, the children, in receiving nourishment. This the woman accepts. She is conscious of her poverty; she claims no rights and privileges. But, aware that the Jews have been fed by Jesus, she asks for the crumbs which are left over from the meal. She shows great faith and humility, and Jesus responds graciously. The Gentiles are, in fact, to be fed. He heals her daughter 'from afar'. The boundaries are transcended.

Jesus continues his journey, following a rather unusual route, passing through the predominantly Gentile region of Decapolis. There he cures a man who is deaf and has a speech impediment. The Gentile people enthusiastically and perceptively acknowledge what he has done, expressing themselves in language which recalls Isaiah's messianic prophecy about the deaf hearing and the dumb speaking (Isaiah 35:5-6). It is in this Gentile setting that Mark locates the second multiplication story.

> *1* In those days when there was again a great crowd without anything to eat, he called his disciples and said to them, *2* "I have compassion for the crowd, because they have been with me now for three days and have nothing to eat. *3* If I send them away hungry to their homes, they will faint on the way – and some of them have come from a great

distance." *4* His disciples replied, "How can one feed these people with bread here in the desert?" *5* He asked them, "How many loaves do you have?" They said, "Seven." *6* Then he ordered the crowd to sit down on the ground; and he took the seven loaves, and after giving thanks he broke them and gave them to his disciples to distribute; and they distributed them to the crowd. *7* They had also a few small fish; and after blessing them, he ordered that these too should be distributed. *8* They ate and were filled; and they took up the broken pieces left over, seven baskets full. *9* Now there were about four thousand people. And he sent them away. *10* And immediately he got into the boat with his disciples and went to the district of Dalmanutha (8:1-10).

The opening phrase '*in those days*' maintains the link with Gentile territory. The great crowd of people who have been accompanying Jesus for some days have come '*from far away*', an expression used of Gentiles in the Old Testament (Joshua 9:6,9; Isaiah 40:4). Jesus is moved by compassion again, but this time his compassion is focused on the people's physical hunger. The initiative here lies with Jesus rather than with the disciples. The latter question the possibility of obtaining bread in such a location; they seem to have forgotten the earlier incident. Jesus is informed that they have some bread, seven loaves. There is no mention of fish at this point. Jesus gets the people to sit. His actions recall the first multiplication: he takes the loaves, says the blessing (this time the verb *eucharistein* is used), breaks them and hands them to the disciples for distribution. Again the disciples are involved. The allusion to the Last Supper and the community's celebration of the eucharist is emphasised in this version by the late mention of the few small fish, which then receive a separate blessing and distribution. A double blessing was not part of a formal Jewish meal, and so the presence in the narrative of a further blessing suggests to some scholars that the feeding miracle has been assimilated to Jesus' actions at the Supper, where Jesus pronounces a blessing over the bread and give thanks over the wine (14:22-23).

The narrative concludes with the collection of the leftovers, which fill seven baskets. A different word is adopted here for the baskets (*spuridai*), a term without any specifically Jewish connotation. Other echoes of Jewish background have been muffled in this second story, such as references to the Exodus and shepherding. The perspective opened by the encounter with the Syro-Phoenician woman has developed further. Having fed a crowd of Jews, Jesus has now fed a group of Gentiles with more than crumbs, and there are leftovers for the future. The word which describes the crowd is no longer exclusive; it is best translated 'people' rather than 'men', as in the earlier feeding story. [4]

Mark's readers would have understood these two narratives as pointing to their eucharistic celebration in which they meet the Risen Lord and anticipate the messianic banquet. Many scholars believe that Mark's presentation is intended as a challenge for his community, in which there is resistance to joint eucharistic fellowship. Despite their reluctance the disciples are called to provide nourishment for both Jew and Gentile; this is their responsibility.

As the narrative continues to unfold, the same structural pattern is maintained. There is a crossing to the mysterious Dalmanutha, another controversy in which the Pharisees demand a sign from Jesus, a request which he decisively rejects. Another boat journey follows, or perhaps the original journey interrupted by the insertion of the controversy is continued. The topic of bread again arises. This time the disciples are deeply concerned because they have only one loaf with them. Jesus reprimands them, for, in their hardness of heart, they run the risk of becoming like the Pharisees of the previous incident.

> 17 And becoming aware of it, Jesus said to them, "Why are you talking about having no bread? Do you still not perceive or understand? Are your hearts hardened? 18 Do you have eyes, and fail to see? Do you have ears, and fail to hear? And do you not remember? 19 When I broke the five loaves for the five thousand, how many baskets full of broken pieces did you collect?" They said to him, "Twelve."

20 "And the seven for the four thousand, how many baskets
full of broken pieces did you collect?" And they said to
him, "Seven." 21 Then he said to them, "Do you not yet
understand?" (8:17-21)

Jesus upbraids them for their failure to understand the meaning of the
two occasions when he has fed the crowds. Sadly, they do not perceive
who Jesus is; they do not understand the nature of his mission.
The evangelist is challenging his community to recognise Jesus' presence in their midst in their eucharistic celebration, and to recapture the
true nature of their sharing in his mission, remembering his providing
nourishment for both Jew and Greek alike. Just as the original disciples
need to have their eyes opened, so Mark's community needs to be
rescued from the dangers of blindness, narrowness of vision, restrictive
practices, and hardness of heart.

THE LAST SUPPER

ALL THE GOSPELS describe the final meal which Jesus had with his
disciples. The setting is the feast of Passover, a celebration recalling
the Exodus and therefore pregnant with theological significance in
terms of liberation, covenant, the gathering of a people, hope in a
future. Mark suggests that Jesus' final meal is the Passover meal.
(5) After the anointing at Bethany (14: 3-9), Judas approaches the
religious leaders with an offer to assist them in their plan to arrest
Jesus (14:10-11). Mark then writes:

On the first day of Unleavened Bread, when the Passover
lamb is sacrificed, his disciples said to him, "Where do you
want us to go and make the preparations for you to eat the
Passover?" (14:12)

Jesus gives the disciples detailed instructions, which they carry out.
'They prepared the Passover.' In Mark's account of the Last Supper,
Passover details are minimal, consisting in the sharing of a cup of
wine and the reference to the covenant. The focus is on Jesus' words
and actions over the bread and cup. The narrative reads as follows:

17 When it was evening, he came with the twelve. *18* And when they had taken their places and were eating, Jesus said, "Truly I tell you, one of you will betray me, one who is eating with me." *19* They began to be distressed and to say to him one after another, "Surely, not I?" *20* He said to them, "It is one of the twelve, one who is dipping bread into the bowl with me. *21* For the Son of Man goes as it is written of him, but woe to that one by whom the Son of Man is betrayed! It would have been better for that one not to have been born." *22* While they were eating, he took a loaf of bread, and after blessing it he broke it, gave it to them, and said, "Take; this is my body." *23* Then he took a cup, and after giving thanks he gave it to them, and all of them drank from it. *24* He said to them, "This is my blood of the covenant, which is poured out for many. *25* Truly I tell you, I will never again drink of the fruit of the vine until that day when I drink it new in the kingdom of God." *26* When they had sung the hymn, they went out to the Mount of Olives. *27* And Jesus said to them, "You will all become deserters; for it is written, 'I will strike the shepherd, and the sheep will be scattered.' *28* But after I am raised up, I will go before you to Galilee." *29* Peter said to him, "Even though all become deserters, I will not." *30* Jesus said to him, "Truly I tell you, this day, this very night, before the cock crows twice, you will deny me three times." *31* But he said vehemently, "Even though I must die with you, I will not deny you." And all of them said the same (14:17-31).

Mark's structure is powerful. (6) It contains three episodes, two at the Supper itself, and a third as Jesus and his disciples leave the supper room for the Mount of Olives. Jesus speaks about the coming betrayal to be perpetrated by one of the group of the Twelve, a friend and table companion, who partakes of the same dish (Psalm 41:9). He then speaks words over the bread and cup. As they leave the supper room after the meal and concluding psalms, Jesus, in shepherding language recalling Zechariah (13:7), foretells the scattering and flight of all the disciples and the denials of Peter. In the tragedy of it all there is a note of hope as he promises that he will later lead them into Galilee. The inadequacy and failure of the disciples, his close friends, chosen to be 'with him' (3:14), serves as the framework for the words and action of Jesus which express his deep self-giving love. This structural feature highlights the significance of the central event and the contrast between Jesus and his disciples. It also shows that Mark's agenda includes both the self-giving of Jesus and the fate of his disciples.

Jesus takes the bread, says the blessing, breaks the bread and gives it to the disciples (as in the multiplication narrative). This gesture was a feature of any formal meal, and it established the fellowship of those taking part. In this Passover context, Jesus interprets the action, giving it a new meaning: *'Take it; this is my body.'* It is the sign of his self-giving unto death for others, a sign of his person and his mission; it expresses the deepest meaning of who he is and what he is about.

Later Jesus takes a cup of wine, again gives thanks, and gives it to the disciples for them to take a drink. After they have drunk, he again interprets what is happening: *'This is my blood, the blood of the covenant, poured out for many.'* Blood poured out is a clear indication of violent death. Reference to the blood of the covenant recalls the Exodus, and the relationship between God and the people ratified by blood (Exodus 24:8). Jesus defines the meaning of his coming death as a sacrificial shedding of blood, the means whereby the covenant relationship with God will be renewed and brought to a new level of fulfilment. This relationship is not restricted to the Jews, but is *'for many'* (Isaiah 53:12), a semitism denoting 'all', an inclusive saving outreach. The phrase recalls and explains the words of Jesus earlier in the narrative:

> "For the Son of Man came not to be served but to serve, and
> to give his life a ransom for many" (10:45).

Drinking the wine is the way in which people participate in the effects of his death and in the blessings of this covenant. Partaking of the bread and wine at this table establishes profound fellowship with Jesus, and creates a new community. A disciple who will betray, a disciple who will deny 'being with', and a group who will run away, drink of this cup, as the faithful Jesus includes them in the offer of God's mercy and love.

Finally, Jesus solemnly declares that this is his last meal until he shares in the final banquet of the Kingdom, the coming of which is intimately associated with his death as the eschatological prophet. In the midst of pending failure and suffering and death, there is a note of hope and victory. As in the three 'passion predictions' earlier in the story, Jesus, the Son of Man, trusts that the Father will vindicate him, that love will have the last word, and that the Kingdom will be finally established. His confidence includes his fragile disciples, for the vindicated Shepherd will lead them into Galilee (14:28; 16:7).

Although in Mark's narrative of the event there is no command to '*do this in memory of me*', as in Luke (22:19) and Paul (1 Corinthians 11:24-25), it is clear that the ritual and language of the eucharistic celebration in the Marcan community lie behind his presentation. Future disciples, Jew and Gentile, beyond prejudice and divisions, share table fellowship with the Lord, and, as members of the new covenant people, share the Kingdom banquet. The striking symbolism of bread broken and given and wine spilled for others reminds them of the meaning of Jesus' life and death, and challenges them to make that their life pattern. The way of Jesus is the way of his followers (8:34-35). Future disciples also share this table in fragility, failure and brokenness. Jesus remains the compassionate and faithful shepherd.

The Gospel of John

THE LAST SUPPER

JOHN'S PRESENTATION OF THE LAST SUPPER is different from that of the other Evangelists. It covers five chapters, which contain farewell discourses and the final prayer of Jesus. Surprisingly, despite its length there is no explicit mention of the institution of the eucharist, the words and actions of Jesus over bread and cup. But there is material which is of interest for our theme, particularly in chapter 13. There are two major episodes in this chapter: the washing of the disciples' feet and the gift of the morsel to Judas. Most scholars treat the rest of the chapter (verses 31-38) as part of the first discourse which follows, but these verses also contain a reference to Peter's denials, and are thematically and structurally linked with the Judas incident.

In chapter 1, when discussing the foot-washing in connection with baptism, it was noted that the general setting is the celebration of Passover, even though in this Gospel Jesus' final supper is not a Passover meal, since it takes place on the previous day. We also touched on other themes: the coming of the 'hour', the love of Jesus for his own and the concluding of his life's work (13:1-2). The act of self-giving service whereby Jesus washes the disciples' feet is a sign of his coming self-giving in death. Jesus tells them that they are to repeat in their lives what he has done for them (13:13-15). Some scholars see here a eucharistic significance also. [7] Instead of including the words over the bread and cup, the institution of the eucharist, John sets out to describe what the eucharist means in the life of the Christian community. Not only does it make present the self-giving death of Jesus. It also challenges us as participants to make real in our daily lives the self-giving and service of Jesus, to copy his example. Liturgical celebration cannot be divorced from the reality of daily living.

The section which runs from verse 21-36 contains the other two aspects of the Marcan Supper narrative which we have just considered: Jesus' prediction of betrayal by Judas and denial by Simon Peter.

21 After saying this Jesus was troubled in spirit, and declared, "Very truly, I tell you, one of you will betray me." *22* The disciples looked at one another, uncertain of whom he was speaking. *23* One of his disciples – the one whom Jesus loved – was reclining next to him; *24* Simon Peter therefore motioned to him to ask Jesus of whom he was speaking. *25* So while reclining next to Jesus, he asked him, "Lord, who is it?" *26* Jesus answered, "It is the one to whom I give this piece of bread when I have dipped it in the dish." So when he had dipped the piece of bread, he gave it to Judas son of Simon Iscariot. *27* After he received the piece of bread, Satan entered into him. Jesus said to him, "Do quickly what you are going to do." *28* Now no one at the table knew why he said this to him. *29* Some thought that, because Judas had the common purse, Jesus was telling him, "Buy what we need for the festival"; or, that he should give something to the poor. *30* So, after receiving the piece of bread, he immediately went out. And it was night (13:21-30).

John's version is more elaborate and dramatic than that of Mark. The pain and anguish of Jesus at the prospect of betrayal by one sharing the sacred intimacy of his table is openly expressed. There is the short dialogue between Simon Peter and the disciple enigmatically referred to as 'the one whom Jesus loved', and the uncertainty and confusion amongst the other disciples. Satan enters into and takes control of Judas, who departs into the darkness of the night, a darkness which is both real and symbolic.

The central action is that Jesus dips a morsel of bread into the dish, 'takes it' (according to some manuscripts), and gives it to Judas. Twice it is stated that Judas receives the piece of bread. This language recalls the earlier bread miracle (6:1-15) and the Supper tradition of the Synoptics and Paul. In verse 18, as a prelude to the Judas incident, John quotes Psalm 41:10: '*He who eats bread with me has turned against me*'. This psalm is reflected also in Mark 14:18 and Luke 22:21; it probably formed part of the early tradition about the Supper. But the

Fourth Evangelist replaces the normal Greek verb for 'eat' with one which means 'to munch' or 'to crunch with the teeth', the verb which he uses in the explicitly eucharistic material of 6:54-58. Consequently, there are some scholars who see the giving of the morsel as having eucharistic overtones. It is an expression of Jesus' self-giving love for his disciple, despite the evil which is in his heart. (8)

After Judas' departure, Jesus triumphantly proclaims his imminent glorification, which will take place through his being *'lifted up'*. He then speaks affectionately to his *'little children'*, telling them that he is shortly to leave them. He continues:

> 34 I give you a new commandment, that you love one another.
> Just as I have loved you, you also should love one another.
> 35 By this everyone will know that you are my disciples, if you
> have love for one another" (13:34-35).

His love for them has been manifested in his washing their feet and giving the morsel – expressions of unconditional self-giving. His parting commandment spells out the way in which his disciples are to conduct themselves after his departure; they are to love one another after the pattern of his love for them, and in this way continue his lifestyle.

Jesus then replies to Simon Peter's claim to be willing to give his life for him by solemnly predicting his denials. It is precisely in his love for disciples who fail that Jesus shows that he is the revelation of the love of God. This is the Evangelist's message for his community as in their fragility and brokenness they encounter the presence of the Risen Lord in their eucharistic celebration.

In passing, it is worth noting that in the Gospel of Luke, one of the special features of his presentation of the Last Supper is the theme of service. Luke recounts the institution of the eucharist first, and then moves on to Jesus' prophecy of Judas' betrayal. This is followed by a dispute amongst the disciples at the table about which of them is the greatest. To this Jesus responds with a statement and a brief parable:

> 25 But he said to them, "The kings of the Gentiles lord it
> over them; and those in authority over them are called
> benefactors. 26 But not so with you; rather the greatest
> among you must become like the youngest, and the leader
> like one who serves (Luke 22:25-26).

These words turn normal expectations, hopes and practice upside
down. Jesus presses his point home with the parabolic saying:

> For who is greater, the one who is at the table or the one
> who serves? Is it not the one at the table? But I am among
> you as one who serves (22:27).

Jesus is the Master, the host at the table, but his habitual style
throughout his ministry has been to attend to the needs of others.
This is the meaning of his body *'given for you'* and his blood *'poured
out for you'*, a meaning which his disciples seem incapable of understanding and accepting. His words echo an earlier parable:

> 36 Be like those who are waiting for their master to return
> from the wedding banquet, so that they may open the door
> for him as soon as he comes and knocks. 37 Blessed are
> those slaves whom the master finds alert when he comes;
> truly I tell you, he will fasten his belt and have them sit
> down to eat, and he will come and serve them (12:36-37).

This culturally astounding role reversal, which in context probably
refers to the parousia or second coming, is anticipated in John's
description of the Supper.

THE BREAD OF LIFE

THE NEAREST WE COME to the words of eucharistic institution in
John's Gospel is in the discourse material of chapter 6. After the multiplication of the loaves and fishes, the crowd recognise through that
sign that Jesus is the prophet who was to come into the world, and

they attempt to make him their messianic king. This is an indication that they do not understand his true identity and role, so Jesus escapes from them, and takes to the hills. The disciples get into the boat to cross the lake, and Jesus comes to them as they struggle with the wind and strong sea. The inclusion of this incident, which is found also in Mark, as we have seen, breaks the narrative flow in John. This is an indication that the two stories were linked at an early stage in the tradition. Jesus identifies himself to his fearful disciples as 'I am', a clarification which ought to dispel the previous misunderstanding about his true identity. Next day Jesus gives a discourse in the synagogue at Capernaum, a discourse which draws out the significance of the feeding. This discourse is usually referred to as the discourse on the Bread of Life.

The Old Testament background is strong. The people demand a sign from Jesus to authenticate his claims, suggesting as a standard of comparison the great miracle of Moses in providing manna in the desert, the bread from heaven. They provide a scriptural quotation in corroboration: *'He gave them bread from heaven to eat.'* The subsequent discussion is based on this text, and deals firstly with the phrase *'he gave them bread from heaven'* (v.32-48), and then considers the verb *'to eat'* (v.49-58). Jesus insists firstly that it was God not Moses who provided the people with manna in the desert. The rabbis had come to interpret manna as the Law, which was understood as a source of revelation and life. Jesus now claims that he is the Bread from heaven, a source of nourishment which satisfies hunger and slakes thirst in a way which the Law could never do. The image of 'bread from heaven', 'bread of life', indicates the revelation which Jesus brings, a revelation which surpasses the Law. Jesus knows the mind and heart of God and has been sent to make this God known. Those who respond in faith to the revelation he brings will not die like the desert wanderers; they come to share now the life of God, 'eternal life', a quality of life which cannot be extinguished by death, but will endure for ever.

Towards the end of the discourse there is a change, and a new element is introduced. *"The bread that I shall give for the life of the world is my flesh."* Jesus will make God known, will reveal God, not only by his teaching, but also by an unconditional gift of himself in death so that the world might have life.

> 51 I am the living bread that came down from heaven. Whoever eats of this bread will live forever; and the bread that I will give for the life of the world is my flesh." 52 The Jews then disputed among themselves, saying, "How can this man give us his flesh to eat?" 53 So Jesus said to them, "Very truly, I tell you, unless you eat the flesh of the Son of Man and drink his blood, you have no life in you. 54 Those who eat my flesh and drink my blood have eternal life, and I will raise them up on the last day; 55 for my flesh is true food and my blood is true drink. 56 Those who eat my flesh and drink my blood abide in me, and I in them. 57 Just as the living Father sent me, and I live because of the Father, so whoever eats me will live because of me. 58 This is the bread that came down from heaven, not like that which your ancestors ate, and they died. But the one who eats this bread will live forever." (6:51-58)

The saying recalls 3:15, which we considered in chapter one:

> 14 And just as Moses lifted up the serpent in the wilderness, so must the Son of Man be lifted up, 15 that whoever believes in him may have eternal life. 16 For God so loved the world that he gave his only Son, so that everyone who believes in him may not perish but may have eternal life.

The language is now unmistakably eucharistic: bread, bread which is flesh, blood, the invitation to eat and also to drink, giving, for the world. These words reflect the eucharistic celebration of the Johannine community, and recall the image of the Shepherd who lays down his life for the sheep (10:15). They also echo the Supper terminology of the Synoptics and Paul. The theme of Jesus as revealer and life-giver has a fresh focus, for it is his violent death, indicated in the separation of flesh and blood, his being 'uplifted' when the 'hour' comes, that is the climax and high point of his revealing and life-giving. For the evangelist, it is in the community's celebration of the eucharist that the revelation of God and the sharing in God's life are encountered and deepened, because the eucharist celebrates and makes present the 'uplifting' of Jesus. [9]

This section also highlights the effect of such eating and drinking: we abide in him and he in us. This language of reciprocal indwelling and profound intimacy between Jesus and the believer will be further developed in the image of vine and branches (15:1-17). The believer is drawn into the relationship which exists between the living Father and the Son whom the Father has sent. The eucharist sustains the oneness brought about by baptism and the gift of the Spirit, the oneness between us and Jesus and the oneness we share with each other as a communion/community. We share such intimacy now, share the very life of God, 'eternal life', and Jesus guarantees the fullness of life beyond physical death in resurrection. [10]

The Resurrection Narratives

ONE OF THE FEATURES of several of the resurrection narratives is that the encounter with the Risen Jesus takes place in the context of a meal, and the meals have eucharistic overtones.

LUKE AND EMMAUS

THE EMMAUS STORY is one of the most beautiful narratives in the New Testament, a literary gem. [11] It takes up the themes of journey and meal, both prominent in Luke's telling of the Good News of Jesus. As the narrative unfolds, it becomes clear that the two disciples, perhaps man and wife, despite the women's story of the empty tomb and the angel's message and Easter proclamation, have turned their backs on Jerusalem and left the other members of their group. They are hurrying away, disillusioned, disappointed, in grief and unbelief. Their hopes and dreams are shattered, their expectations dashed, their future an empty void.

A stranger suddenly breaks into their lives and into their tragedy, and walks their way with them. They capitalise on the opportunity to tell him their story and articulate their anguish and distress. But they fail to recognise him. Luke dramatically prolongs the element of non-recognition common to the appearance narrative pattern. The stranger then seeks to enlighten them at some length on the basic scriptural paradigm of suffering leading to glory which underlies his own experience. The narrative continues:

> 28 As they came near the village to which they were going, he walked ahead as if he were going on. 29 But they urged him strongly, saying, "Stay with us, because it is almost evening and the day is now nearly over." So he went in to stay with them. 30 When he was at the table with them, he took bread, blessed and broke it, and gave it to them.
> 31 Then their eyes were opened, and they recognised him; and he vanished from their sight. 32 They said to each other, "Were not our hearts burning within us while he was talk-ing to us on the road, while he was opening the scriptures to us?" (24:28-32).

The conversation has enthralled them and drawn them out of their self-absorption, so that they can feel concern for the stranger in need of food and shelter. They invite him in, and he accepts. As has hap-pened so often in his ministry, Jesus eats with broken people. He reaches out and touches them in their failure and disloyalty, their fragility and inadequacy, and breaks with them the bread of reconcil-iation and friendship. That outreach in table fellowship transforms their understanding and reshapes their lives. They recognise him in the breaking of the bread. Then, with a spring in their step and a smile in their eyes, they set out without delay to retrace their route to Jerusalem, and to share their experience and news with the others.

Luke is proclaiming that as the Christian community celebrates the eucharist in failure and brokenness, we can encounter the Risen Jesus today in the breaking of the word and the breaking of the bread.

When the two disciples rejoin the others, they learn that the Lord has reached out to Simon in a similar way, extending to him too his forgiveness and companionship. As they all talk together Jesus appears in their midst and they share a meal of fish. In this meal context Jesus then commissions them to preach forgiveness to the nations, forgiveness which they have experienced profoundly in their table fellowship with him.

JOHN AND TIBERIAS

THE OTHER POST-RESURRECTION NARRATIVE with eucharistic echoes is found in John. It is the appearance of the Risen Lord as a stranger on the shore of the Sea of Tiberias. After the appearance of the Risen Jesus in Jerusalem, the giving of the Spirit and the commissioning of the disciples (20:19-23), which we considered earlier, it comes as a surprise to find them in Galilee, back at work with their boats and nets. The story has the hallmarks of a first appearance. It is best to view this as an independent narrative from the Galilee resurrection appearance tradition, which was added to the original Gospel before its divulgation, and was written by a different author of the Johannine school. Perhaps it is a version of the tradition of the appearance to Simon referred to in 1 Corinthians 15:5 and Luke 24:34.

Simon and a small representative group of disciples have spent a fruitless night fishing in their familiar lake. In the early morning light Jesus is present on the shore, but is not recognised by them. They heed his word and obey his suggestion that they make another attempt on the starboard side, and make a catch so large that they cannot haul it in. The beloved disciple is again the first to recognise Jesus: '*It is the Lord*'. Simon jumps into the water and swims ashore whilst the others bring in the boat and the catch. The focus of the narrative then switches from the catch to the meal.

9 When they had gone ashore, they saw a charcoal fire there, with fish on it, and bread. 10 Jesus said to them, "Bring some of the fish that you have just caught." 11 So Simon Peter went aboard and hauled the net ashore, full of large fish, a hundred and fifty-three of them; and though there were so many, the net was not torn. 12 Jesus said to them, "Come and have breakfast." Now none of the disciples dared to ask him, "Who are you?" because they knew it was the Lord. 13 Jesus came and took the bread and gave it to them, and did the same with the fish (20:9-13).

Again it is a scene of reconciliation and forgiveness, for the charcoal fire is a reminder of the charcoal fire near which Simon Peter denied Jesus (18:18). Again there is a meal of bread and fish, provided and prepared by Jesus. The action of Jesus, as he takes the bread and gives it to them, and then does the same with the fish, recalls the earlier sign of the loaves and fishes, which took place by the same lake. Unlike the Emmaus story, the disciples here recognise Jesus prior to his breaking the bread. The eucharistic motif and background are evident. The readers would link this lakeside story with their own eucharistic experience.

Another interesting and significant detail in the narrative is the fact the net containing the large number of fish does not break despite the quantity. This symbolises the universality and unity of the Christian community. It picks up the symbolism of the undivided garment in the Calvary scene (19:23-24). The eucharist, like the mission of Jesus, has a great deal to do with unity. For some, the fishing aspect, in which Simon Peter takes a leading role, is an indication of the disciples' future mission, the success of which is dependent on the presence and help of Jesus. This mission or commissioning element of the pattern of resurrection narratives is developed later, when Simon is given the opportunity to make amends for his threefold denial. Reconciled and rehabilitated, he is given the role of shepherd and instructed to feed the sheep.

Paul

THE TRADITION

THE EARLIEST PRESERVED WRITTEN TRADITION about the celebration of the eucharist is found in the first of Paul's letters to the community of Corinth, dated 55 AD. [12] In this letter Paul is addressing a number of issues which have arisen in that Church, some reported to him by letter, others by word of mouth. Amongst these is the problem caused by divisions and factions, some of which become stridently present when the community gathers for the celebration of the Lord's Supper. Such gathering usually took place in the home of a fairly wealthy member. There was a meal prior to the Lord's Supper, and possibly a further service of prayers, readings and hymns afterwards. It appears that some select members of the community arrived first and partook of a rather lavish meal, sometimes to excess, whilst others, probably the slaves and the poor, who were obliged to work longer hours, arrived later and found little or nothing left to eat. Another contributory factor may have been the structure of the house. The dining room proper (the *triclinium*) had space for only a few; the rest were obliged to occupy the larger hall or courtyard (the *atrium*). Thus the social and economic divisions already present in a community which was far from homogeneous, (consisting of rich and poor, male and female, free and slaves, Jews and Greeks), were underscored in the setting of the Lord's Supper. There were haves and have-nots, advantaged and disadvantaged, first and second class members, an inner group and the rest. For Paul such disunity, and the selfishness and lack of concern it manifests, contradicts the meaning of the Lord's Supper and is quite unacceptable.

It is in an attempt to remedy this situation that Paul reminds them of the tradition which he handed on to them previously when he was first with them in person at the founding of the community, around 50/51.

23 For I received from the Lord what I also handed on to you, that the Lord Jesus on the night when he was betrayed took a loaf of bread, 24 and when he had given thanks, he broke it and said, "This is my body that is for you. Do this in remembrance of me." 25 In the same way he took the cup also, after supper, saying, "This cup is the new covenant in my blood. Do this, as often as you drink it, in remembrance of me." 26 For as often as you eat this bread and drink the cup, you proclaim the Lord's death until he comes (1 Corinthians 11:23-26).

The language of receiving a tradition and handing it on is a technical formula used by Jewish rabbis and Greek philosophers, where important teaching and practice was faithfully and authoritatively communicated from generation to generation. The tradition which Paul recalls is not his own creation; he had himself received it at the time of his own conversion and instruction (between 30 and 34). It goes back to the earliest days of Christianity, and probably reflects the liturgical practice of the Christian community in Antioch.

Paul roots the tradition in the historical events which took place *'on the night that Jesus was handed over'* – not just by Judas and the religious leaders, but by God, as part of God's saving plan. On that occasion there was a significant meal at which Jesus (referred to from the post-resurrectional perspective as 'Lord') did and said certain things.

Paul's version is different from that of Mark in a number of respects. The actions of Jesus follow a similar pattern: he took bread, gave thanks to God, broke it and said, *'This is my body'*. Paul omits the detail that he gave it to them, though this is clearly implied. His tradition adds the phrase *'which is for you'*, possibly reflecting Isaiah 53:12, and the injunction *'Do this in remembrance of me'*. It is clear that an interval followed, and it is after supper that Jesus speaks over the cup. Unlike Mark's version, no gestures accompany his words. Jesus' declaration over the cup is more diffuse: *'This cup is*

the new covenant in my blood', and lacks the simple identification of
the contents of the cup with the blood of Jesus, which is found in
Mark. The theological explanation *'poured out for many'* is also
absent. The two share a reference to the Covenant, but Paul describes
this covenant as *'new'*, possibly under the influence of Jeremiah 31:31.
Paul's tradition again includes the injunction to repeat the action in
Jesus' memory, which provides some balance between the two sets of
words, and probably reflects the influence of liturgical practice.
However, there is no further attempt to balance the ritual of the bread
and the narrative words about the cup, which is not ritualised. It is
generally agreed that we have here a very early form of the eucharistic words and actions attributed to Jesus, even if every detail may not
go back to the Last Supper. [13]

The idea of 'remembering' is a key concept in Jewish liturgy. It does
not mean simply to recall. Remembrance expresses trust, gratitude
and worship. According to the Semitic mentality, participants share
in the effects of the saving events which are remembered; they
become contemporary with the events and are drawn into them.
The identity of the individual and of the community are shaped by
the significant, often foundational events which are ritually remembered. There is also a looking forward to final eschatological
consummation with its new possibilities for transformation.

This eschatological dimension is reflected in v.26, which is probably
not part of the original tradition, but is a Pauline comment. The
words and gestures of the Lord's Supper proclaim the saving death
and resurrection of Jesus. This points onwards to his coming again in
glory, when we shall celebrate the final messianic banquet, as our
story reaches its culmination.

The remembering of the death and resurrection of Jesus in the Lord's
Supper makes demands on the participants, for they are drawn into
his humility and self-giving love for others. To remember demands
imitation. *'Do this in remembrance'* implies both liturgical celebration and a self-giving and unifying lifestyle. This is the challenge for

the community at Corinth, and Paul goes on in v.27-33 to spell out the implications for them in language with a judicial ring. The kind of behaviour perpetrated shows that they are partaking of the eucharist in an unworthy manner, and this merits the Lord's judgement. Their conduct and the attitudes it displays give the lie to what the Lord's Supper proclaims and celebrates. They are told to examine themselves, to scrutinise their conduct, if they are to avoid God's condemnation.

The tradition which Paul puts on record in this letter is invaluable for attempts to recover the earliest tradition and to get near to the actual words of Jesus at the Last Supper. His purpose, though, is to clarify the meaning of the Christian celebration, and to draw out the implications for Christian living, so that the Christians of Corinth will live in a way which harmonises and integrates with what they celebrate.

STRONG AND WEAK

The full implications of Paul's message become clearer when we recall his words earlier in the letter. Another issue which was creating division stemmed from the pagan environment within which the fledgling church was established. Some members of the community were partaking of meat which had been offered to idols, and perhaps even taking part in pagan temple banquets which were part of the cultural life of the city. They saw no problem in this because, as liberated Christians, they knew that idol worship was meaningless and eating such meat had no religious implications. However, this was a source of offence to others, who were in danger of being drawn into such practices against their conscience, and so becoming embroiled in idolatry. There was also an arrogance about the former type of community member, referred to as the 'strong' and enlightened, who ignored or looked down on the others, the 'weak' and vulnerable (8:1-13). For Paul there can be no compromise with idolatry, and freedom must be relinquished for the sake of concern for others, which is the greater value. This is explained by our oneness with and in Christ.

16 The cup of blessing that we bless, is it not a sharing in the blood of Christ? The bread that we break, is it not a sharing in the body of Christ? *17* Because there is one bread, we who are many are one body, for we all partake of the one bread (1 Corinthians 10:16-17).

Central aspects of Paul's eucharistic theology are found here. The term translated as 'sharing' is the word *'koinonia'*, which, as we saw in the chapter on baptism, means communion or common union. Partaking in the bread and cup brings about a oneness with the Risen Christ, and also a deep mutuality with one another beyond natural divisions (Galatians 3:28). Together we are one in Christ. The baptismal union is strengthened, experienced and manifested. Anything which threatens this profound oneness contradicts what is being remembered and celebrated.

The words of Jesus, which Paul recalls, express his self-giving in love. Remembering this, making this present again through the signs of the bread and the wine, is a challenge to live accordingly. Behaviour which militates against unity is out of place in the context of eucharist. For Paul it is necessary to live the oneness which the eucharist celebrates and proclaims. 'Doing this' implies both the liturgical celebration and a self-giving and unifying lifestyle. As disciples we proclaim the Lord's death until he comes both by liturgy and by life. When Paul goes on to speak of eating and drinking unworthily, he is referring to the anomaly of celebrating a symbol of oneness whilst living in a manner which is divisive.

Conclusion

A NUMBER OF STRANDS have clearly threaded their way through the material which we have been considering. They can be drawn together, I believe, by the key symbols associated with eucharist.

ONE TABLE, ONE BREAD, ONE CUP

CALLED TOGETHER BY THE GIFT OF GOD, we gather around one table and share one bread, one cup. The eucharist reveals and expresses the ongoing saving and liberating love of God, who continues to seek and find us, offering us forgiveness, acceptance, healing, and life. Table fellowship remains such a powerful symbol.

The eucharist reveals what we are as Church, as Christian community: a people brought together from many different 'places' (different in age, sex, colour, nationality, social status, education...), with different stories and different gifts. The eucharist is a profound expression of unity in the richness of diversity. We are one with the Risen Jesus, who continues to be present with us as our Emmanuel, and continues to 'pitch his tent' in our midst as faithful shepherd and loving friend. In him we are united with one another in the depths of our being. We are one in the mystery of God's love, bonded and enlivened by the Spirit, able to acknowledge God as 'Father'. We are one with our world as we use in our celebration such materials as bread, wine, water, light, metal, wood, stone, cloth, art, dance, music, and flowers, drawing them into the new creation.

However, several of the texts which we have considered confirm our own experience that being true to our personal and shared Christian identity provides a challenge. We are aware of our own poverty and need, our brokenness and failures, our economical love. We are conscious of unity strained and fractured, of diversity which has degenerated into divisiveness in vision and outlook, attitude and practice. The symbol of one table, one bread, one cup, which synthesises the Christian ideal, is therefore a striking challenge.

One of my favourite books puts it this way: *"Life drawn from the eucharist makes all kinds of demands on you to proclaim the meaning and greatness of this mystery. You are called especially to give the sacrament its full effect in unity, brotherhood and service. The unity of all Christians and all people must be closest to your heart. Always and everywhere you are called to rise above oppositions and divisions in the universal love of Christ. Always look for what unites, and fight everything that estranges and separates people from each other."* [14] To celebrate eucharist, then, is a dangerous thing, for it entails the practical resolve to strive in our daily lives at a personal and communal level to realise ever more completely the unity of which it is a sign. It commits us to live in love, acceptance, hospitality, reconciliation, service, genuine friendship. Otherwise our celebration is an empty gesture, a hollow shell. Eucharist cannot be a lush oasis, a segment excised from the circle of daily life. It gathers into one loaf our daily efforts to support and upbuild and unify; it celebrates this; it sends us forth in the strength of that bread to continue to strive for the fulfilment of the Lord's dream and prayer *'that they may be one'* (John 17:21). One area of particular challenge highlighted by our texts is the availability of table fellowship for the 'sinners' and marginalised.

BREAD BROKEN AND WINE OUTPOURED

THE OTHER FUNDAMENTAL SYMBOL is the bread broken and the wine poured out. This was the gesture through which Jesus interpreted the whole significance of his life and death, his surrender in love and trust to the Father and to mission. This symbol reminds us that *"the celebration of the Eucharist would be nothing but a romantic or aesthetic sensation should you forget that the heart of it is the self-giving of Jesus."* [15] The eucharist draws us into the mystery of the 'hour' of Jesus, his love to the uttermost through which we are saved.

To celebrate eucharist is to accept the implications of discipleship, to fashion our lives in accordance with the sign of the broken bread and poured wine. To celebrate eucharist is to commit oneself to a growing oneness with the Jesus who gives himself, to commit oneself to his way of self-giving and service, to the sharing with others of all we have received from his tenderness and love, to the washing of others' feet. Self-sacrifice for the sake of others is the only foundation upon which community can be built. We cannot forget the words of the Master: *"A grain of wheat remains a solitary grain unless it falls into the ground and dies; but if it dies, it bears rich harvest"* (John 12:24). The eucharist sends us out to break the bread of our lives, to pour out our gifts and energy in the service of others, especially those in need.

NOTES

(1) In addition to the commentaries referred to in chapter 1, note 3, see E. LaVerdiere, *The Eucharist in the New Testament and the Early Church* (Collegeville, Liturgical Press 1996); F.J. Moloney, *A Body Broken for a Broken People* (Melbourne, Collins Dove 1990); J. Meier, "The Eucharist at the Last Supper: Did it happen?" in *TD* 42:4 (Winter 1995), p.335-351.

(2) See, for instance, Job 9:8; Habakkuk 3:15; Psalms 77:17-21; 29:3; 65:7; 93:3-4; 107:23-30; Isaiah 51:9-10, 15; 43:1-13.

(3) J.P. Meier, *A Marginal Jew*, vol 2, p.922-924. His treatment of the episode runs from 905-924.

(4) For this view of a provision of food for Jews and then for Gentiles see the commentaries of Harrington, Moloney, McBride. M.D.Hooker argues strongly against this interpretation.

(5) Many scholars are of the opinion that, whilst the overall setting is that of the Passover celebration, Mark has turned the final meal into a Passover meal for theological reasons. They hold that John's version, in which the meal takes place the evening before Passover, is historically more likely to be correct. See the detailed treatment of the issue in J.P. Meier, *A Marginal Jew*, vol 1, p.386-401; R.E. Brown, *John*, vol 2, p.556.

(6) This structure forms the centrepiece of the wider balanced structure of 14:1-72. See F.J. Moloney, *A Body Broken*, p.30.

(7) See J.P. Meier, *The Eucharist*, p.343-344.

(8) See F.J.Moloney, *John*, p.383-384; *Body Broken*, p.93-99.

(9) After the death of Jesus his side is pierced by the soldier's lance and blood and water flow out. Many scholars understand this as symbolising the sacraments of baptism and eucharist through which the new life obtained by Christ becomes available for believers. Again John links eucharist and cross.

(10) I refer the reader to the commentaries on John mentioned in chapter 1, note 8.

(11) In addition to the commentaries on Luke (chap 2, note 10) and the books on the Resurrection recommended in chap 1, note 12, see R.H. Fuller, *The Formation of the Resurrection Narratives* (London, SPCK 1972); B. Rigaux, *Dio l'ha Risuscitato* (Milan, Edizioni Paolini 1976); X. Leon-Dufour, *The Resurrection and the Message of Easter* (London, Chapman 1974).

(12) See F.F. Bruce, 1&2 *Corinthians* (London, Oliphants 1971); R.F. Collins, *First Corinthians* (Collegeville, Liturgical Press 1999); J. Murphy-O'Connor, *St. Paul's Corinth. Text and Archeology* (Collegeville, Liturgical Press 1983); A.C. Thiselton, *The First Epistle to the Corinthians* (Carlisle, Paternoster Press 2000).

(13) Matthew's wording is similar to that of Mark. He adds the injunction to 'eat' in the bread word. Prior to the cup word in Mark there is a statement that they all drank from the cup. Matthew makes this the introduction to the cup word: 'Drink from this, all of you...' He thus creates a better balance and parallel between the two sets of words than does Mark. Matthew adds 'for the forgiveness of sins' to the cup word, a

phrase which recalls Joseph's dream in 1:21. Luke's version seems to be basically the Pauline tradition with some influence from Mark. There is much scholarly discussion about the original words of Jesus which lie behind these liturgical traditions. A classic on the subject is J. Jeremias, *The Eucharistic Words of Jesus* (London, SCM 1966). J.P. Meier, (*The Eucharist*, p.347) concludes his analysis by suggesting that the earliest form of the narrative was: he took bread, and giving thanks (or: pronouncing a blessing), broke (it) and said: 'This is my body.' Likewise also the cup, after supper, saying: 'This cup is the covenant in my blood.'

(14) *Rule for a New Brother* (London, DLT 1973), p.30-31.

(15) *Rule*, p.29.

Conclusion

IN THE COURSE OF THIS BOOK we have limited our scriptural enquiries and considerations to passages which have bearing on the sacraments of baptism, confirmation, reconciliation and eucharist. Our endeavours have provided enormous enrichment. From a literary point of view we have seen some of the differences in the style of the various authors, and noted such techniques as irony, symbolism, double meanings, parallelism. We have examined a wide range of different types of literature: discourses, letters, miracle stories, narratives, parables, poetry, prophetic utterances. We have become more sensitive to the importance of context, and to the influence of the Old Testament. We have become more aware of the part played by the experience of the early Christian communities and the creativity of the authors in the formation of the texts. We have become aware of some textual difficulties. We have also encountered some historical issues, amongst them the problems arising in Paul's churches, the different traditions concerning the location of resurrection appearances and the variations in

the wording of the commissions, the different
versions of the words of Jesus over the bread
and wine at the Supper, and the question
whether that Supper was a Passover meal.

The emphasis, however, has been placed on the wealth of theological
insights which the texts offer, insights which are not speculative but
practical and life-enhancing. The texts outline key elements of what
I would call a sacramental spirituality. They tell us about our
Christian 'being' and identity and how we should live this out. They
reveal the amazing depth of our relationship with God as children
who share God's life. They proclaim our shared being in Christ, our
fundamental communion with one another as Church, enlivened by
God's Spirit of love. They enable us to understand better the person
of Jesus, his mind-set and values, the way he viewed his mission and
surrendered to it with trust and love. They remind us that, as bap-
tised/confirmed people, we are called to witness and empowered to
mission, for we have responsibilities to the wider world, and they
suggest a range of ways in which we can articulate this mission.

The texts which we have considered celebrate the fact that we are
reconciled people, and accept our ongoing need for forgiveness and
healing. They recognise that we gather for the breaking of the word
and the breaking of the bread, and inculcate that we seek to live what
we celebrate, striving for unity and peace. They make it clear that the
faithful following of Jesus is demanding and costly, but assure us that
he remains with us, sustaining us with his life. In short, they place
before us a vision which is stimulating and exciting, and which embraces every aspect of our being and human experience. They invite
us to develop our potential as individuals and as Church, and to
become ever more fully alive.

Scripture indeed sheds light on the sacraments and opens up a sacramental way of living, a spirituality. May the Lord Jesus set our hearts
on fire as he continues to walk our way with us.

Michael T Winstanley, a member of the Salesians of Don Bosco, is a graduate of the Salesian Pontifical University (Rome) and London University. He is currently Director of Savio House, a Retreat Centre near Macclesfield, Cheshire. He also lectures in Biblical Studies at Ushaw College, Durham. He has spent many years in Formation Ministry, served a term as Provincial of the British Province, given retreats in many countries, and been involved in a variety of adult education programmes. This is his third book.

The author invites us to revisit the scriptural roots of our contemporary sacramental experience. Using the techniques and insights of modern biblical scholarship, he examines a wide range of passages which have bearing on the sacraments of baptism, confirmation, reconciliation and eucharist. He draws out their literary characteristics, notes some of the historical issues, and seeks above all to reflect on their theological message. The texts offer an outline of a sacramental spirituality, an exciting and challenging way of living our Christian discipleship in today's world.